Houses of Heart Pine

To Glenda Bailie,
with best regards,
Pharris D. Johnson

Houses of Heart Pine

A Survey of the Antebellum Architecture of Evans County, Georgia

Pharris DeLoach Johnson

Published under the auspices of the
Evans County Historical Society

Printech
Glennville, Georgia

Houses of Heart Pine
A Survey of the Antebellum Architecture of Evans County, Georgia

by Pharris DeLoach Johnson

Copyright © 2001 Pharris D. Johnson

Library of Congress number: 01-130780

ISBN: 09658544-1-8

First Edition

Book design: Linda Hester and Stephanie Durrence; Cover design: Pharris Johnson and Benjamin Mautner.

Published under the auspices of The Evans County Historical Society, P.O. Box 6, Claxton, Georgia 30417.

Frontispiece: View from an upstairs window of Evans County's antebellum Smith-Daniel House.

Front Cover Photo: A.D. Eason House.

Back Cover Photos: Architectural details from antebellum houses in Evans County, Georgia. *Clockwise from top left*: hand-wrought latch, Durrence House; column capital, Eason House; antique key, Berry Brewton House; split-rail fence, Berry Brewton House; shutters, Simon Brewton House; wooden hinges, Durrence House; strap hinge with eyelet, Durrence House; shutter, Smith-Daniel House; *Center,* log corncrib, Durrence House. (Photos by author.)

To my cousin and friend

John P. Rabun, Jr.

"By wisdom
a house is built,
and by understanding
it is established..."

Proverbs 24:3

TABLE OF CONTENTS

ACKNOWLEDGMENTS

It is indeed a pleasure to thank the people who helped me on this project. I am very grateful for their invaluable assistance and encouragement.

The basis of this publication is my thesis submitted for a Master of Arts degree in historic preservation at the Savannah College of Art and Design. Professors Hector Abreu and Dr. Daves Rossell served on the thesis committee. Professor Abreu, an eminent authority in historic preservation, was my thesis committee chair and Professor Rossell, an expert in vernacular architecture, gave superb support as a topic consultant. Professor Rossell also provided encouragement to pursue publication of this survey. Computer art Professor Tan Tascioglu rendered valuable assistance with restoring several vintage photographs.

Much appreciation goes to the following individuals who assisted with the survey of the houses: Margaret Eason, Paul Eason, and Tim Eason, (A.D. Eason House); Warren Wilbanks, Reggie Wilbanks, and Gene Berry, (Benjamin "Berry" Brewton House); George and Susan Willcox, and Cleta McCorkle, (Brewton-Hendrix House); Carroll Anderson, (Simon J. Brewton House); Debra and Wayne Purcell, and Byron Hair, (Thomas A. Durrence House); Gene Strickland, J.C. and Julia Strickland, and Drefus Strickland, (Edwards-Strickland House); Eileen Walters, (John Rogers House); Walter Emmett Daniel, Emmett Daniel, Jerry Griner, (Smith-Daniel House); and Janean Coe and Bobbie Todd, (Thomas E. Rogers House). Their help contributed greatly to my research and to the successful completion of the fieldwork.

Other people who graciously shared information for the project include: Pat Cooper of Athens; Kemp Mabry of Statesboro; Mary Frances Oliver of Glennville; Mark Baxter of Macon; Ray DeLoach of Savannah; and Evans County residents Wallace Parker, Emily and David Groover, and Peter Strickland. Mr. Strickland contributed information on the Simon J. Brewton House, the Edwards-Strickland House, and antebellum architecture in the area. Al Hackle, editor of *The Claxton Enterprise*, kindly published an article soliciting information on the houses in the survey.

My sister, Linda Hester of Thomasville, provided assistance with the page layout and served as my editor. Connie Pinkerton, of Savannah, expertly assisted with the editing task. John Rabun, Jr., a Tattnall County native who resides in Atlanta, read the manuscript and provided excellent suggestions for improvements. He also contributed significant information on the Brewton-Hendrix House. Dorothy Simmons, a local historian in Evans County, served as a topic consultant and provided superb help in developing the manuscript. I am especially thankful for the steadfast encouragement of these individuals during this project.

Several of the people mentioned above also provided documents and photographs to aid my research. The photo and document captions identify these much-appreciated contributions.

Stephanie Durrence, of Printech, provided cheerful and competent assistance with the publication production process. It is always a pleasure to work with Bill Werkheiser, the owner of Printech.

A special thank you goes to JoAn Strickland and Dorothy Simmons of the Evans County Historical Society for their support in publishing this work. The Society is active in preserving the history of the county and JoAn and Dorothy readily recognized the importance of documenting its antebellum architectural legacy.

Above: The Pridge Beasley
log house depicted in one of
the few extant vintage
photos of an antebellum log
structure in Evans County.
The house was razed in the
early twentieth century.
Right: Luke Pridge Beasley
and wife, Jemima Rowe
Beasley. (Photos courtesy
of Ga. Dept. of Archives and
History)

INTRODUCTION

Though small in number, the antebellum houses of Southeast Georgia's Evans County provide some notable examples of vernacular rural architecture. Despite the existence of these relatively rare structures, there has never been a comprehensive survey of them. This publication seeks to fill that void.[1]

Evans County, located approximately 50 miles west of Savannah, is one of Georgia's more recently formed counties. In August 1914, the Georgia General Assembly created Evans County from the southwestern part of Bulloch County and the northeastern end of Tattnall County. In addition to the county seat of Claxton, the towns of Evans County include Daisy, Hagan, and Bellville. Each of these towns began in 1890 with the establishment of railroad service through the area.

AREA HISTORY

The once-frontier territory that is now Evans County was very sparsely populated in the first decades of the nineteenth century. The county's only river, the Canoochee, served as an early travel route and pioneers first settled along its banks.

This area was known as the Pine Barrens or flatwoods part of Georgia. Nearly level topography with sandy loam and sandy topsoils characterize the land. Comprising the lower southeast half of the state, the soils have generally high water tables and are well adapted to timber production and pastures.

The first residents were primarily subsistence farmers who also raised livestock. These settlers came mainly from the Carolinas and the parts of Georgia settled in the eighteenth century. The homes of this era were no doubt only semipermanent and none of these first settlers' structures remain. However, by the mid-1800s several of the area's plantation owners had accumulated enough wealth to build sturdy, if not elaborate, rural homes.

Built in 1857, the Tattnall County Courthouse was one of the few high-style buildings in antebellum Georgia's Pine Barren counties. (Drawing by A. K. Singley. Courtesy of Mark Baxter)

The immediate area was devoid of any high-style, grand architectural structures, civil or residential, until construction of the Tattnall County Courthouse in Reidsville in 1857. Built by George Merriman and John Pearson, the structure was classic Greek Revival. This was the only such building in the county for decades to come.[2]

After 1865, the white residents of Tattnall and Bulloch counties struggled to recover from the social and economic devastation brought on by the war. African Americans faced new problems in making a living for their families as laborers or sharecroppers. During the postwar period the residents continued to rely on traditional crops and livestock production. There was little new house construction until the 1870s and most dwellings were of modest proportions.

The railroad arrived in what is now Evans County in 1890, after which the area experienced significant growth. In the decade between 1890 and 1900, the Tattnall County population almost doubled, growing from 10,253 to 20,419.[3]

After the turn of the twentieth century, the predominant house form was the single-story, single-pile, central-hall type. These dwellings typically had ells behind the front part of the house. The formerly detached kitchens were now connected via an ell or breezeway.

By the 1920s, the bungalow became an increasingly important house type in the county's towns and rural areas. The hall-and-parlor cottage also remained popular.

Today, agriculture still dominates Evans County's economy. Much of the housing stock reflects the rural environment, but contemporary dwellings coexist with traditional housing types. One needs only to travel the county's primary and secondary roads to see an eclectic blend of old and new.

ARCHITECTURAL SURVEY

This publication documents a survey and examination of Evans County's remaining antebellum homes. The list of these pre-War Between the States structures is regrettably short. The small geographic size of the county, combined with the lack of preservation efforts in the first half of the twentieth century, limits the number to only nine.

The first phase of this survey included reviewing all known historical references to antebellum houses in the county. Among these were Lucile Hodges's classic work on Evans County history, *A History of Our Locale*, and the excellent recent book, *A History of Evans County, Georgia*, compiled by Dorothy Simmons. Additional resources included area newspapers, manuscripts, and various other books cited in the bibliography.

In 1983, the Altamaha-Georgia Southern Regional Development Center conducted an Architectural and Historic Properties Survey/Inventory of Evans County. The house descriptions provided by this inventory, however, were summary in nature and did not give sufficient details to be of substantial use in the current study.

The local newspaper, *The Claxton Enterprise*, published an article on this survey and solicited input from residents having information relating to the county's antebellum homes. This advertisement provided several important leads for information and acquisition of vintage photographs of the houses.

Evans County Antebellum House Locations

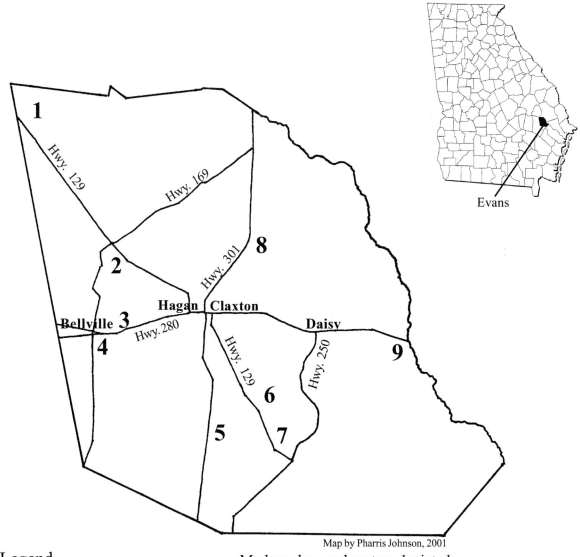

Map by Pharris Johnson, 2001
Modern-day road system depicted.

Legend
1. A. D. Eason House
2. Brewton-Hendrix House
3. Berry Brewton House
4. Smith-Daniel House
5. Thomas A. Durrence House
6. John "Duffy" Rogers House
7. Thomas E. Rogers House
8. Simon J. Brewton House
9. Edwards-Strickland House

After the determination of the probable antebellum houses (or in one case early 1860s house), the project's second phase began. This phase consisted of a field survey of each of these houses. This work included conducting oral interviews with the current owners, physical examination of the houses to determine prior alterations, and a review of construction materials and methods used. This survey, in turn, helped date the houses more precisely through each structure's form and materials.

A review of courthouse records provided information on chains of title to the land, tax records, estate returns, and other key documents. If the approximate date of the house construction could not be verified through reasonable physical and documentary evidence, the house was not included.

The research results revealed that there are nine antebellum residential structures remaining in Evans County. These houses are the following: the Smith-Daniel (southeast corner of intersection of Highways 280 West and 169 in Bellville) and "Berry" Brewton (approximately 100 yards north of the intersection of Highways 280 and 292 in Bellville); the Edwards-Strickland House (2.2 miles east of Daisy on south side of Highway 280 East); the Brewton-Hendrix House (west side of Highway 129 North, 3.8 miles north from intersection of Highways 280 and 129 in Claxton); the Simon J. Brewton House (100 yards east of Highway 301 north, 3 miles north of Claxton); the Thomas A. Durrence House (.5 mile east on Tom McCall Road [County Road 59] off Highway 301 south); the John "Duffy" Rogers House (.3 mile east on Rogers Road [County Road 81], off Highway 129 South); the Thomas E. Rogers House (.2 mile east on Arlie Todd Lane [County Road 259], off Highway 129 South); and the A. D. Eason House (1.1 miles north on A.D. Eason Road [County Road 2], off Highway 129 North), in Undine.

There are other architecturally significant early structures in the county. There are three houses on the National Register of Historic Places in addition to the Evans County Courthouse in Claxton and the Glisson Store in the Evans County portion of Ft. Stewart. The three houses on the register are the Mitch Green House (1878), northeast of Claxton on the southeast corner of the U.S. 301 and Ga. 169 intersection; the Dr. James W. Daniel House (1910), on Newton Street in Claxton; and the George W. DeLoach House (1892) in Hagan. These fine homes and other nineteenth-century area dwellings such as the W. W. Daniel (1895) and Augusta Elders (1876) houses in Bay Branch, among others such as the restored 1870s log cabin of Bill and Pat Boney, form a rich architectural heritage for the county. These structures are, however, post-War Between the States and these later-vintage houses will hopefully be the subject of a detailed countywide survey conducted at a future date.

By way of overview, the first chapter of this book outlines the history of the Plantation Plain type house in Georgia. The Plantation Plain is the most prevalent antebellum structure type remaining in Evans County. Chapter Two provides information on the antebellum building process in Evans's parent counties of Tattnall and Bulloch. The other chapters provide the results from the surveys of the extant antebellum houses in the county. The only way to fully understand the history of these houses is to examine the lives of the owners. Accordingly, the house chapters include biographical information on the original occupants.

Each of the house chapters contains a floor plan. Solid black walls indicate the original configuration of the house and are based on the architectural investigation conducted during this survey. Later additions are indicated by wall partitions without the black fill.

The photographs used in this publication came from various sources including individuals cited in the Acknowledgments, other publications, and the author's files. Several were from the American Historic Building Survey as published in *The Architecture of Georgia* by Frederick D. Nichols. Photographs without credit lines were taken by the author in 2000 and 2001 for this survey.

The goal of historic preservation, as related by the Secretary of the Interior's Standards, is to "protect and preserve materials and features that convey the significant history of a place." Hopefully, this research, inventory, documentation, and interpretation will highlight an important part of the county's history and spur interest in preserving its architectural heritage.[4]

1 THE PLANTATION PLAIN HOUSE IN GEORGIA

Of the nine Evans County houses in this study, six are frame and three are log construction. Five of the frame structures are the Plantation Plain architectural type. Of the others, one is a double-pile or massed form and the original part of three are of traditional log house construction. Because of the predominance of the Plantation Plain house in the county's antebellum building inventory, this chapter will examine the origin and diffusion of the type in the state.[1]

A definition of the terms *type*, *style*, and *form* as used in this publication is important. These terms are easily confused. The house type relates to the overall form and layout of rooms, whereas style refers to the external ornamentation. For example, the shotgun type house of one room wide and two or more rooms deep could have Colonial Revival details. A Plantation Plain type structure could have Federal or Greek Revival stylistic features. The terms *type* and *form* are used interchangeably.[2]

The most frequent house type in this study is Plantation Plain. Georgia builders constructed houses of this form from the late 1700s to the 1870s. *The Georgia Preservation Handbook* gives this type its own separate architectural category due to its prevalence in the state and because it "was the basic 'root stock' on which Federal and Greek Revival architectural styles were grafted." Since the *Handbook* uses the Plantation Plain name, that term is used in this book.[3]

According to the handbook:

> A definition of Plantation Plain can best be described by its silhouette and plan. Found in almost all parts of Georgia, this two-story gabled roof form has a one-story front shed porch and shed addition on the rear with two exterior end chimneys. In plan the house is generally a two-over-two room design but often also is found to have a center hall.[4]

Figure 1.1
Carter's Quarters, Murray County

Figure 1.2
Traveller's Rest, Stephens County

Figure 1.3
Tullie Smith House, DeKalb County

Examples of

Plantation Plain

Houses in Georgia

Figure 1.4
Eagle Tavern, Oconee County

Figure 1.5
Henderson-Fore House, Jasper County

Figure 1.6
Dell-Goodall House, Screven County

Figure 1.7
Murray House, Long County

Figure 1.8
Bacon-Fraser House, Liberty County

Photo credits: Figures 1.1, Historic American Buildings Survey.; 1.5, Kenneth Kay; others by author.

The Plantation Plain type has several other names outside of Georgia. Among these are the Southern I-house, Carolina I-house, Virginia I-house, extended I-house, I-house with porch, I-house with shed, North Carolina farmhouse with shed porch and lean-to, Piedmont house, and Federal Plain-style.[5]

Architectural historian Frederick Doveton Nichols first applied the Plantation Plain name to this house type in his 1957 book, *The Early Architecture of Georgia.* He even declared a "Plantation Plain" period in the architecture of Georgia. Nichols describes this era as beginning in the Early Republic (1790-1819) and continuing into the Greek Revival (1820-1860) period.[6]

Although Nichols was the first to use the term "Plantation Plain," Harold Bush-Brown discussed this vernacular house type in a mid-1930s Historic American Building Survey-sponsored review of architecture in Georgia. Brown referred to these houses as "the usual farmhouse" category between "the pioneer cabins and the more pretentious plantation homes."[7]

The Plantation Plain form is a subtype or derivation of the I-house. The evolution and dispersal of the I-house is the subject of considerable research. The geographer Fred Kniffen in his definitive work *Folk Housing: Key to Diffusion,* identifies the I-house as one of the most widely distributed dwelling types in the eastern and mid-United States. Kniffen dubbed the form "I-house" because of its commonality in Indiana, Illinois, and Iowa. The "I" was also a symbol for the tall, slender frame that characterizes these houses.[8]

Kniffen traced routes of diffusion showing various forms of the house type emanating from New England, Middle Atlantic, and Lower Chesapeake hearth areas. From these locations the type extended to most of the eastern United States. Settlers from the Middle Atlantic area carried the plan to the Midwest and South. The form had variations across its area of dispersal. The I-house in Virginia was sometimes brick, and did not have the full-width front porch prominent in the lower South. Most Virginia and lower South I-houses had exterior-end chimneys. In the Midwest, however, the chimney was normally in the interior of the house.[9]

Kniffen summed up his observations on the I-house saying:

> From section to section the I-house varied in construction
> material from brick and stone to frame and logs. Chimneys
> might be central, inside end, outside end, or paired on the
> ridge, with regional dominance of specific practices. The floor
> plan was to be highly variable. Lateral and rear appendages,
> front and rear porches, galleries, even classical columns ap-
> peared in great variety. But these qualities all I-houses unfail-
> ingly had in common: gable to the side, at least two rooms in
> length, one room deep, and two full stories in height. These
> constant qualities, a continuous distribution, still-extant logical
> evolutionary states, and almost exclusive association with eco-
> nomic success in an agricultural society dictate a common
> fundamental concept and thus describe a type. The few es-
> sentials constitute the basic type, beyond which there are sev-
> eral varieties.[10]

Though the I-house is usually associated with rural dwellings, there
are several urban examples. The Charleston single house is really an I-house
with its narrow end facing the street. The I-house type is present in prominent
Georgia antebellum towns such as Washington, Milledgeville, and Savannah.
In Savannah (Fig. 1.14), there are several excellent examples around the city's
Washington Square area. A common variation with the Savannah I-houses is
the presence of paired dormer windows and raised basements.

Architectural historians have not studied the Plantation Plain structure
in proportion to its importance. Rather, they leave the examination of the type
to the cultural geographer and local historian. The neglect may be a result of
its more mundane vernacular form being less favored than the grander high
styles.

Despite the wide popularity of the I-house type, however, not all
observers agreed with the merits of the design. In his 1804 description of the
ideal country dwelling, agriculturist William Cobbett declared the I-house plan

(Fig. 1.9) unsuitable for rural surroundings because it was built for the excesses of urban life. As he put it, this house was a "rural absurdity" and "all show and little use." He preferred the single-story cottage and cited their advantages of increased stability in high winds, simplicity of chimney cleaning, and easier access in extinguishing accidental fires. Cobbett failed to realize the importance these dwellings would achieve with a few simple modifications adapting the form to life in the South.[11]

GEORGIA'S ANTEBELLUM RURAL LANDSCAPE

The belief that the large plantation house dominated the rural landscape of the antebellum South is a myth. The majority of planters were middle-class, yeoman farmers. With much of their capital tied up in slaves and land, most of them struggled to run profitable operations. Though less romantic than the image of the Old South Greek Revival plantation dwelling, the housing for the average planter was usually plain and simple.

The Plantation Plain structure was well suited to the conditions and housing needs of Georgia, and it became very popular. The house had many features to accommodate the warm and humid climate. To help with ventilation on the upper floor, the form allowed placement of windows on three sides

Figure 1.9
Agriculturist William Cobbett used this sketch to depict the urban house he felt unsuitable for the country. No doubt he would have been surprised by the house type's later popularity. (From *An Epitome of Mr. Forsyth's Treatise of the Culture and Management of Fruit Trees.*)

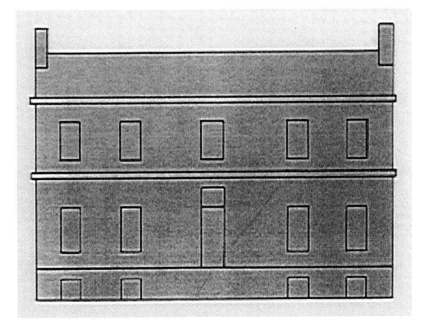

of each room. Other features of the type suitable to the climate included high ceilings, floors raised three or more feet off the ground, roofs with steep pitches, wide porches, large windows and doors, and a wide central passage in later examples.

These houses sometimes included a small room on one or both ends under the porch roof. These were often known as the "parson's room" or "prophet's chamber" because they provided ready and separate accommodation for traveling preachers or other visitors. The lean-to rear shed portion of the house was one-room deep. These back rooms were typically smaller than those in the main part of the house and extended across the full width of the structure.

Yet another facet of this house type's popularity was the visual image it created. The second story projected imposingly upward and the facade provided an impression of largeness. In effect, these rather plain houses *looked* larger than they really were. This pretentious aspect of the structure was made-to-order for the local gentry comprised of upper middle-class planters. The ample facade created an appearance of economic well being. This image was even more pronounced when the house faced the road, as was typically the case. Additionally, the extensive porches and large windows and doors projected the sense of hospitality that was so prevalent during the era.

As the middle-class planters attained sufficient wealth and increased the size of their families, they needed larger dwellings. However, full-fledged mansion houses were beyond their means and the smaller, one-story hall-and-parlor or raised cottage dwellings were not large enough to comfortably accommodate the large families typical of the era. The Plantation Plain house was the answer in that it was easily expanded over time. The owner could attach wide front columns on the porch for style and add a second floor to a single-story, hall-and-parlor cottage configuration to accommodate the need for increased space.

The "two-over-two" room plan allowed four rooms under one roofline in the main section of the house. As a practical matter, this configuration made construction simpler and cheaper when compared to linear or massed single-story rooms. The roof need only cover half of the area required by a four-room ground floor footprint. Another feature was the energy efficiency available via exterior-end single chimneys that could house both upstairs and down-stairs fireplaces. Additionally, its dominant side-gabled roof along the width of the house was not only a relatively easy roof type to build, but its framing also created one of the strongest roofs available due to its efficient dispersion of loads.

The full-width front porch not only provided a practical place for living in the extreme heat of Georgia, but also added to the harmony and openness of the structure. The porch proved a cooler location to perform household duties and allowed for social activities. These wide porches distinguish the Plantation Plain subtype from its cousins in Virginia and the "I" states. Typically, I-house porches in those locations cover only the front entrance. The long-galleried porch concept originated in the West Indies and came to Georgia via North and South Carolina.[12]

One distinguishing feature of the front porch changed over time. Most of the older Plantation Plain porch roofs have flat vertical ends even with the plane of the walls of the house. Later examples have half-hipped porch roofs.

Another distinction of the later houses is that they typically have roof returns at the bottom of the eaves of the main body of the house. The steepness of the pitch of the rear shed lean-to also varied. The flatter-pitched configurations allowed window placement in the back of the second-floor rooms. However, the steeper lean-to porch roofs in some later examples provided a higher ceiling for the rooms, but insufficient space to place windows on the backside of the second floor.

GEORGIAN ARCHITECTURE'S INFLUENCE ON PLANTATION PLAIN HOUSES

The Plantation Plain house in the state of Georgia followed a natural evolutionary development. These structures emanate from the English Georgian house form so popular from 1700 to 1780, and later in some areas. Georgian architecture strongly influenced house building in the South during the late eighteenth and most of the nineteenth century.[13]

The Georgian structure grew from the Italian Renaissance via England, and the name emanates from the three King Georges who reigned in the eighteenth century. In England this Renaissance classicism was widely popular from 1650 to 1750. This architecture type typically consisted of one- or two-story boxes, two rooms in depth, and symmetry of doors and windows. The Georgian influence is apparent in the I-house, and Georgian houses in Great Britain have striking similarities to those in America.[14]

English colonists brought their architectural preferences with them to America, and assimilated the Georgian house form into the culture. Colonial American builders augmented their knowledge of this type architecture by reading building manuals or pattern books. These volumes continued as standard references into the antebellum period and included such works as Owen Biddle's *Young Carpenter's Assistant* and Asher Benjamin's *American Builder's Companion* and *Practical House Carpenter*.[15]

Essentially, Plantation Plain form was the front half of the Georgian massed-plan house. Similarities included the side gable, windows matched horizontally and vertically, and paired exterior-end chimneys. The adaptation of this type in Georgia and other southern states included the previously mentioned full front-width porch and rear shed rooms.[16]

The Plantation Plain house type may also reflect influences from the Southern coastal hall-and-parlor cottage in that it applied a second floor onto a form that already had a gable roof, shed porches, and symmetrical door and window configurations.

PLANTATION PLAIN PERIOD IN GEORGIA

The first Plantation Plain houses appeared in Georgia at the end of the eighteenth century and continued through most of the nineteenth century. Built with readily available longleaf yellow pine, middle-class plantation owners constructed these houses in significant numbers throughout the state. Despite the longevity of the house type, proportions did change over time.

Among the earliest extant and restored Plantation Plain houses in the state are the Thornton House (c. 1790) at Stone Mountain Park, Eagle Tavern in Watkinsville (c.1795-c.1820), the Parker-Callaway House (1800) at Callaway Plantation in Washington, and the Dell-Goodall House in Sylvania (c. 1810). These earlier period houses have the pronounced vertical and more delicate profile associated with the Federal style prevalent between 1780 and 1820. The eighteenth-century houses do not have front full-width porches or rear shed rooms as found on later examples. On the early nineteenth-century houses with wide porches, the columns are typically narrow.

State historians note that the Thornton House (Fig. 1.10) at Stone Mountain, moved from its original location in Green County, is one of the oldest restored houses in the state. The builder, Redman Thornton, was of English ancestry, and moved to Georgia from Virginia in the late 1700s. The house is story-and-a-half and the dwelling's Georgian Period central-hall plan and room configuration identify it as a very early Plantation Plain dwelling. An unusual feature of this house is the nogging construction – a combination of wood framing and brick.[17]

The 1790s Eagle Tavern (Fig. 1.11) in Watkinsville, now a house museum, is another restored example of early Plantation Plain. Its interesting front door arrangement features two doors with separate porches for each entry. One door led into a store and the other into the tavern. The "two-up, two down, Plain style" tavern was a bustling establishment prior to the War Between the States.[18]

The Parker-Callaway House (Fig. 1.12) at the Callaway Plantation, located five miles from Washington, is a notable example of an early Planta-tion Plain. The early 1800s two-story frame house is clearly of the I-house form. It has a "two-over-two" plan with a hall stairway in the hall-and-parlor room arrangement. Moved to its present location from a nearby site in Wilkes County, the house remains virtually unaltered. Like the Eagle Tavern in Watkinsville, the house has two front doors leading into separate rooms.[19]

The Dell-Goodall House (Fig. 1.13) in Sylvania is a very early classic Plantation Plain type. It has a typical vertical Federal profile and three exterior-end chimneys. In addition to the two exterior-end chimneys on the outside of the main gable roof, a second, smaller chimney is attached to the rear shed. It is the lone remaining structure in the former Screven County seat of Jacksonboro. Of note is the faux plaster wainscoting painted on the walls on the upper floor.[20]

Traveler's Rest (Fig. 1.15) in Toccoa is a Plantation Plain form with later lateral extensions. Begun in 1816, the house was originally the residence of pioneer James Wyly. The next owner, Devereaux Jarrett, expanded the structure into one of the finest pioneer hotels in northeast Georgia. The house boasts a 90-foot-long porch and also has hand-numbered rafters. The Georgia Department of Natural Resources now operates a house museum at the site.[21]

In the 1840s the Plantation Plain profiles became more horizontal as seen in the Tullie Smith House (Fig. 1.16) at the Atlanta Historical Center. The Tullie Smith House, with its "parson's room" and surrounding outbuildings, provides an excellent example of the farmstead of antebellum "plain folks."

By the 1850s the horizontal profile became even bolder, and this trend continued into the following decades. Square cased columns replaced smaller timber posts as larger size became more popular with the Greek Revival style.

As the profile became more linear, it allowed for more windows in the upstairs floor. Several of the Evans County examples have five windows on the front and back elevations, with two windows on each gable end. The additional windows provided increased light and contributed to enhanced ventilation for the upper story.

Builders adapted Federal and Greek Revival features to the Plantation Plain structures. Indeed, one of the advantages of this type of house is that owners could add stylistic features to them to make them appear fashionable as trends changed. Federal details included narrow roof overhangs, classical order fanlights, and curved stairways. Among the Greek Revival features were the temple-form portico, two-story porch, and the larger porch columns mentioned above.

In the late antebellum period, central-hall floor plans became more prevalent in the Plantation Plain structure. Halls with rooms on both sides allowed more privacy and marked the transition to more modern house types. The Bacon-Fraser House (Fig. 1.17) in Hinesville is a fine example of the central-hall floor plan.

Gradually some owners and builders expanded the configuration of the second story to more than one-room deep. They needed this configuration not only to accommodate additional rooms, but due to the fact that the large columns on the popular Greek Revival houses would have been out of proportion for a structure with an upper story only one-room deep.

There were many variations of the Plantation Plain plan. Some had two front doors and access to the upper story was normally by interior stairway. In Evans County's A. D. Eason House, the internal stairs lead to the upper porch and entry to the second-story rooms is through outside doors on the porch. At least one example, the Bearden-Chambers House in Madison, has an exterior door in the side elevation next to the chimney.

FORM, FIT, AND FUNCTION

Architect and author Jonathan Hale gives us insight on why building designs developed before the 1830s seem superior to those after that date. Although he does not specifically discuss the Plantation Plain, his observations fit the type perfectly.

Hale says in his book, *The Old Way of Seeing*, "Architecture is the play of patterns derived from nature and ourselves." Using this definition, the proportions of Plantation Plain relate well. The shapes interact pleasingly with each other. The silhouette and visual pattern of the Plantation Plain house provides natural grace and strength. The width, height, and symmetry of the facade provide a sense of stability. The clean, simple lines of these structures give them life.[22]

Hale further states, "What is beyond doubt is the pattern itself [for a structure], the pleasure of organization, color, texture; it is very much like a piece of music." Indeed, if music is the metaphor for architecture, then the Plantation Plain form embraces a graceful, simple melody of order and proportion.[23]

The visual pattern of the Plantation Plain house expressed life in a unique way for the middle-class planter who built it. The long horizontal roofline paralleled the road and echoed the geometry of the outbuildings and fields and provided a sense of order. The regulating, invisible lines created by the proportions and symmetry of the doors, windows, roof, and porch promoted a sense of harmony. The house became a symbol for success. These components combined to make the type perfectly suited to the rural, vernacular setting prevalent across the Georgia landscape.

Summary

Derived from a combination of the Georgian facade and the old English house with an end fireplace, the Plantation Plain type house was the structure of choice for the antebellum middle-class planter. It had many advantages in that it could be built complete or in stages, it was well adapted to the climate, the longleaf yellow pine for its construction was in plentiful supply, and it provided just enough pretentiousness to show attainment of wealth without seeming pompous or overstated.

Although the Plantation Plain house was beyond the means of the small farmers and landless laborers, for the middle-class planter it was a well-received compromise between the unaffordable mansion and the simple cottage or log house. The fact that six of the nine extant antebellum houses in Evans County are of this type speaks to its prevalence in the counties of Tattnall and Bulloch, as well as the other counties of the Georgia Pine Barrens.

Figure 1.10
State architectural historians believe the Thornton House at Stone Mountain State Park is the oldest restored house in Georgia.

Figure 1.11
The Eagle Tavern in Watkinsville is a very early Plantation Plain type structure. Note absence of full-length front porch prominent on later examples.

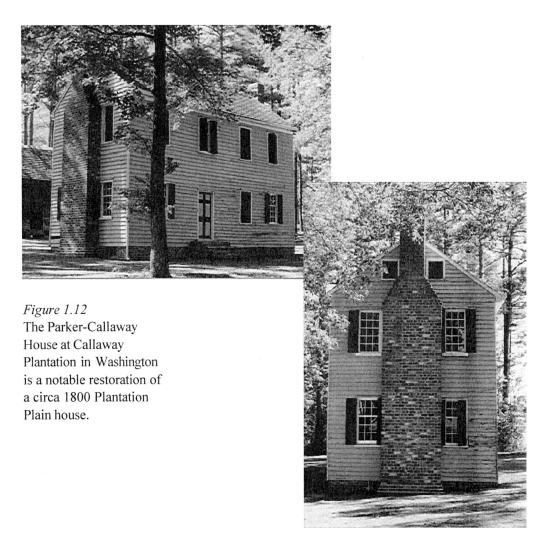

Figure 1.12
The Parker-Callaway
House at Callaway
Plantation in Washington
is a notable restoration of
a circa 1800 Plantation
Plain house.

Figure 1.13
The Dell-Goodall
House in Sylvania
is an early classic
Plantation Plain
structure. Note the
vertical profile
characteristic of the
Federal Period.

Figure 1.14
Although primarily considered a rural house type, city dwellers also used the Plantation Plain form (or I-house with rear lean-to porch). Pictured is the Thomas Williams House at 503 E. President Street in Savannah. This 1808 urban example shows a raised basement and widely spaced, paired dormers. Federal details include a semicircular overlight and a vertical profile of lightness and delicacy. The house lacks the full-width front porch found on later rural examples.

Figure 1.15
Traveler's Rest was
once a frontier hotel
in Toccoa. It is now a
state historic site.

Figure 1.16
The Tullie Smith House
at the Atlanta History
Center provides an
interesting interpretation
of houses of Georgia's
antebellum "plain folks."

Figure 1.17
Hinesville's 1839 Bacon-Fraser House.

Figure 1.18
The c.1803 Hillhouse-
Toombs-Slaton
House in Washington
features a basic
Plantation Plain form
with a wing attached
to each gabled end.

Figure 1.19
The Joseph William Hughs, Sr. House in Long County, built in 1853, has a front porch roof portico reminiscent of Georgian architecture. The detached kitchen is visible in the right rear of the house (*above*).

Figure 1.20
The Dr. Jackson House, Wilkinson County, shows a classic Plantation Plain profile.

Figure 1.21
The Blount-Parks-Mara-Williams House (c. 1818) in Milledgeville has a "two-over-two" with rear shed rooms floor plan. This I-house shows a variation to the full-width porch popular in the later antebellum period.

Figure 1.22
The Major Edward White House (1806) in Milledgeville is a Plantation Plain dwelling with addition of a small portico embellishment above the porch roof.

Figure 1.23
The Harrison-Walker-Brown House in Washington County has a two-story porch attached to a Plantation Plain form. (From *Architecture of Middle Georgia*, by John Lindley. Reprinted by permission of the University of Georgia Press.)

Figure 1.24
One of the Plantation Plain house's advantages was the ease with which it could be modified. At Ogeechee Plantation in Greene County, owner Bo Cheves added a second Plantation Plain house form to the rear of the original structure. This twentieth-century addition created a unique "double I-house."

Figure 1.25
The 1810 Rogers House in Madison shows several generations of modifications. The original "two-over-two" room configuration later had rear shed rooms added. The front porch shows fretwork added to "update" the house in the 1870s.

2 HOUSING IN ANTEBELLUM TATTNALL AND BULLOCH COUNTIES

Diffusion of population and architecture to Evans County came via the same routes as it did to most other counties in the Georgia Pine Barrens. The building forms came from the hearth area of the mid-Atlantic to North and South Carolina and on to Georgia (Fig. 2.1). As cropland in the older states was depleted of fertility and cheap new land became available in Georgia, vast outmigration occurred from the Carolinas. Some of the settlers in the Pine Barrens came after intermediary stops in early Georgia towns and counties and others came directly to the area from other states.[1]

Figure 2.1
This map shows the general dispersion path of the Plantation Plain house to Georgia and Evans County. The architectural type followed the migration pattern of settlers. (Map adapted from *Encylopedia of Southern Culture.* Photos from - Va.: *Virginia Country,* Betsy Edwards; N.C.: *North Carolina Architecture,* Catherine Bishir.)

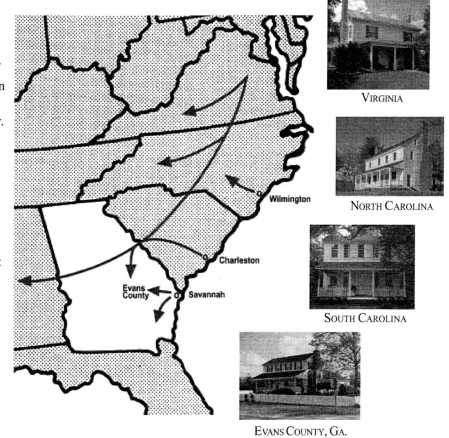

VIRGINIA

NORTH CAROLINA

SOUTH CAROLINA

EVANS COUNTY, GA.

Once an individual decided to build a new house, he had to determine how it would be accomplished. Could he build it himself? What materials were available? Was there a nearby carpenter to employ? Did he or his neighbors have skilled slaves who could assist?

The conservative nature of area planters prompted them to build house types with which they were familiar. The factors that influenced them were the same ones that guide most owners everywhere: availability of materials and labor, ideas from the builder, and suitability of other houses they observed.

It is interesting to note that most of the original owners of the extant Evans County antebellum houses served in public office. Five of the nine owners were at one time members of the Georgia General Assembly. Their travels to the capital in Milledgeville exposed them to architecture elsewhere in the state. Typically they also made at least two visits to the Savannah markets each year to sell their commodities and conduct other business. These trips provided opportunities to view dwellings both in Savannah and along the way. When the time came to construct their own houses, most of these individuals built the Plantation Plain type so popular in the state. The notable exception was A. D. Eason, who built a two-story, two-room deep house on an even grander scale than the others.

Within the immediate area, strong family connections among the sparse population was prevalent. Hence the ideas of preferred house form were easily communicated through visits among the families. One need only review the genealogies of the Brewton, Smith, Durrence, Edwards, Rogers, and Eason families to understand the close family ties that permitted ready exchange of ideas on house styles and other elements of the material culture. The common house forms allowed people to identify with one another.

There were several classes of people in the county during the antebellum period. There were the slaves, landless white laborers, farmers with limited acreage, and the more affluent planters with thousands of acres. Even for the wealthy planters, however, times were not always prosperous. With most of their net worth tied up in slaves and land, they were often strapped for cash.

The Plantation Plain house should not be viewed as the average antebellum dwelling in Tattnall and Bulloch counties. Rather, it was the house of choice of the middle- to upper-class farmer. On the other end of the spectrum of white farmers were those barely eking out an existence, and their more humble houses dominated the landscape. These dwellings were mostly of log construction and rough-cut boards, and many of these were of inferior quality (Fig. 2.2). Some of these structures later had frame additions built to accommodate larger families or were utilized as separate kitchens or outbuildings when new houses were built.

African American slave housing was the most meager of all. There are no Evans County slave dwellings existing today. Nor are there any known descriptions of these houses. However, it is likely they were similar to others in the Pine Barrens that were small, unadorned log cabins.[2]

Figure 2.2
Typical log housing of the Georgia Pine Barrens as drawn by Captain Basil Hall with the aid of his camera lucida in 1828. (From Library of Congress, Prints and Photographs Division)

Many antebellum travelers through the Pine Barrens, of which the Evans area was a part, were unimpressed with the dwellings. Housing for all but the larger planters remained inadequate at best. Editors of the newspapers of the state implored residents to make better use of their resources. William H. Chambers in *Soil of the South*, put it thusly, "A log house half decayed with age, or a framed house without paint, …are too frequently the insignia of the planter's premises."[3]

Chambers also criticized the lack of landscaping in rural Georgia. He described most farmsteads as without so much as a "shrub or flower." It appears that most of the Evans area plantations had modest plantings of varieties such as magnolia, crepe myrtle, gardenias, sweet shrubs, and spirea. Grass lawns were a rarity. For those yards that were maintained, they were "swept" with stiff-bristled booms. The houses had fences around them to keep out animals and add a decorative element.[4]

BUILDING STATISTICS

The building practices of the Evans County antebellum house owners are an interesting case study. As the following table depicts, most of the planters were in their late 20s or early 30s when they built their houses. Most of the men were of above average means, and some of them were among the

EVANS COUNTY ANTEBELLUM HOUSE FEATURES-TABLE 2.1

Name of owner	Date of house construc-tion	Age of owner[5]	Tax value of assets 1860[6]	Acres of improved/ unimproved land 1860[7]	No. of slaves 1860[8]	Origin 1st ancestor to Ga.[9]	Public offices served by owner[10]	Changes in family ownership since con-struction
Abraham D. Eason	1857	41	$23,981	100/4400	24	S.C.	Ga. Gen. Assembly; Tax coll. & rec.	None
William H. Edwards	Before 1846[11]	49 or younger[12]	$17,294	150/7850	23	S.C.	Ga. Gen. Assembly	2
Benjamin "Berry" Brewton	1857/8	26[13]	$3,500	30/470	1	N.C.	Co. tax collector	2
Jonathan B. Brewton	1858	31	$15,169	100/1773	13	N.C.	Ga. Gen. Assembly; Justice of Inf. Court	3
Simon J. Brewton	Early 1850s	Early 30s	$19,630	50/5650	33[14]	N.C.	Justice of Inf. Court; Convention of 1865	None
Thomas E. Durrence	1858	27	$1,366	25/359	None	N.C.	Ga. Gen. Assembly	None
John Rogers	Before 1866	23[15]	None	None	None	N.C.	None	None
James B. Smith	1856/6	33	$7,532	50/2700	2	N.C.	Ga. Gen Assembly; Clerk of Sup. Court	None
Thomas E. Rogers	1858	26	$1,400	20/350	None	N.C.	None	None

Name of owner	Architectural type of house	Size of main part of house (w x l)[16]	Stair location[17]	Chimney configuration	Exterior paint color	Door types	Window sash; 1st floor & 2nd floor[18]
Abraham D. Eason	Double-pile	37' x 28'	Cased, front left room, center wall	Two exterior-end	White	Paneled	6-over-6/ same
William H. Edwards	Plantation Plain, center hall	38' x 27'	Cased, front right room, back wall	Two exterior-end	White	Paneled	6-over-6/ same
Benjamin "Berry" Brewton	Plantation Plain[19]	28' x 28'	Uncased, front room, left front wall	Single exterior-end	None	Batten	6-over-6/ 1 over 1
Jonathan B. Brewton	Plantation Plain	36' x 28'	Uncased, double, one each side of center wall	Two exterior-end	White	Paneled	6-over-6/ same
Simon J. Brewton	Plantation Plain, center hall	45' x 35'	Cased, front left room, center wall	Two exterior-end	Silver-gray[20]	Paneled	6-over-6/ unglazed
Thomas A. Durrence	Plantation Plain, center hall	40' x 26'	Cased, right side, center hall	Two exterior-end	None	Batten	6-over-6/ same
John Rogers	Double-pen (log)	28' x 16'	None	Single exterior-end	None	Batten	6-over-6/ n/a
James B. Smith	1½-story single-pen (log)[21]	31' x 32'	Uncased, front room, right back wall	Two exterior-end	None	Batten	6-over-6/ unglazed
Thomas E. Rogers	Single-pen (log)	24' x 16'	Uncased, right left wall	Single exterior-end	None	Batten	unglazed

wealthiest in the area. Most of them had substantial landholdings. In all cases, the first family settler to the area hailed from the Carolinas. In what seems to be a key to the preservation of their houses until modern times, these dwellings did not often change family ownership.

As seen in Table 2.2, the houses range in size from the relatively modest John Rogers dwelling to the very large houses of A. D. Eason and Simon Brewton. Two of the houses were originally central-hall, four were hall-and-parlor, and two single- and one double-pen. Although the majority were 1850s Plantation Plain form, there was variation of room arrangement.

All nine houses originally had side-gabled roofs, shingle roof covering, and hand-hewn sills. They also show extensive use of heart pine lumber. All of the nonlog houses have weatherboard siding and are braced-frame construction. Additionally, all of the houses faced a nearby road and had wide, full-width front porches.

PROFESSIONAL ARTISANS IN THE AREA

In Evans's parent counties of Tattnall and Bulloch, there was a shortage of skilled builders. The 1850 census lists a Tattnall County white population of 2,378 with only three carpenters, one ship joiner, and no brick masons. Ten years later the white population had increased to 3,153 and carpenters numbered eleven. There were still no masons. Bulloch County, with a population of 2,840 white people could count only five carpenters and no brick masons in 1850. By the end of the following decade the white population totaled 3,495, but there were only six carpenters. However, by that time the county had two "master masons" listed among its inhabitants.[22]

Interestingly, many of these professional artisans were from northern states, where their skills were much more plentiful in the larger cities. Of the eleven carpenters in Tattnall County listed in the 1860 census, five were from Georgia, two from North Carolina, and one each from Massachusetts, New Jersey, Connecticut, and Ireland. Of the six carpenters listed in the 1850 Bulloch County census, one each was from Massachusetts, New York, Maryland, South Carolina, and Georgia, and one of unknown origin. The masons in Bulloch County in 1860 included one from Ireland and one from

Scotland. These artisans were apparently a mobile group also. None of the carpenters identified in the Bulloch and Tattnall county 1850 census remained in the county during the population count ten years later.[23]

Despite a shortage of professionals, there were, however, many laymen with carpentry skills. One needs only to review the estate inventories of the period to see that almost every plantation had a sizable collection of carpenter's tools. Accordingly, the owner could often offer his labor or that of his slaves to the builder. It seems that most enterprising plantation owners had basic carpentry knowledge. Some of the farmers supplemented their income by working as part-time carpenters. In other cases planters rented out their slaves to assist others with construction.[24]

THE TIMBER INDUSTRY

Timber production was important to Bulloch and Tattnall counties throughout the last half of the nineteenth century. Though sparsely populated and devoid of industry, the Pine Barren forest resources of southeast Georgia were immense. Before the railroad was built, timbermen clear-cut the old growth longleaf pines along the riverbanks. They strapped the logs together forming rafts and floated them to market in Darien and Savannah. In Bulloch and Tattnall, rafting took place along the Ogeechee, Canoochee, and Altamaha rivers.

Southern longleaf heart pine has deep roots in America's history and architectural heritage. Until supplies all but disappeared, heart pine was a building material of choice in the South from Colonial times. The first colonists discovered the longleaf pine growing in a relatively small area along the Southeastern seaboard. The 150- to 450-year-old trees grew to 170-feet tall and were up to five feet in diameter. They produced close-grained heartwood that proved to be unexcelled as building material for the times. Heart pine is known for its strength, durability, and beauty. However, these qualities were to hasten the eventual downfall of this prized lumber's availability. Because of the great demand for heart pine, combined with the improper turpentining and reforestation, this valuable resource almost disappeared. Found mostly in protected forests, today less than one percent of the virgin growth longleaf pine remains. The Evans County area was rich with this resource until the turn of the century when the supply began to dwindle. Most of the area's finest historic houses are of this material.

In the *Statistics of the State of Georgia* published in 1849, George White lists Tattnall as having 15 sawmills and Bulloch with 8. There were several mills available to service the residents in the Evans area including ones located on the Canoochee River's Bull, Lotts, and Cedar creeks.[25]

The Brewton Mill on Cedar Creek appears to have been the sawmill of choice for several local antebellum-era builders. Area pioneer Nathan Brewton established the first mill close to the mouth of the creek on the Canoochee River. Later his son, Benjamin, built a second mill further up the creek (Fig. 2.3). Run by waterpower, the mill operated an "up-and-down" or reciprocating saw. The blade on these mills was long and narrow and similar to a crosscut saw. The saw was in a stationary position, and the logs moved on a carriage against it. The blade left straight saw marks that the carpenter later planed from the boards. The mills produced the planks for ceilings, floors, interior trim, walls, and smaller structural members such as rafters. The Brewton Mill changed ownership several times after the War Between the States, converted to steam, and continued operation until the early 1900s.[26]

THE BUILDING PROCESS

Because of the log size, the limitations of local sawmills, and inadequate transportation capabilities, builders hand-hewed the framing timbers for houses at the building site. Typically, they shaped the sills and other large structural members with a felling ax and broadax and smoothed them with a foot adz.[27]

The frame houses were braced structures joined with mortise and tenon. The tenon was a rectangular projecting end that fit into a mortise cavity. This type of construction included a combination of heavy timber frame with hewn joints and four-by-fours for floor supports. The support studs were heavier and therefore not spaced as close together as later "balloon-framed" structures. The carpenters worked with augers, planes, wood chisels, and mallets to shape the mortise holes where precise measuring was necessary to join the tenons. Corner posts normally had up or down diagonal braces (Fig. 2.4). Wooden pegs and trenails secured the joints.[28]

Another laborious process was the production of shingles. Builders cut great tree wheels from cypress logs and then used wedges and mauls to cut triangular blocks from the wheels. Workers then rived the shingles with a froe.[29]

The findings of the present survey indicate that all of the houses examined had shingle roofs initially. The shingles required replacement every 10 years or so. All of the roofs of the survey houses showed common rafters either butted and nailed together or attached to a ridgeplate. The roof framing in all the housing had been rebuilt at some time.[30]

The raising of the house usually required the help of neighbors. The event often included a meal and fellowship afterwards. The house-raisers used ropes and poles to lift the walls so the tenons fitted into the mortised structural framing and remained firm. Workers raised the walls with the tenons fitting in place on the plates so that they endlapped together. The girts were placed atop the studs and the summer beams were trenailed with mauls to lock them in place. The notched rafters were then placed on the wall top plates with spikes or pegs. After completion of these tasks, workers shingled, boarded, and floored the house. The finishing work included the installation of windows, doors and molding, and the hanging of shutters.[31]

The only known antebellum brickmaking yard in the Evans area was at the old town of Palatkee on the Savannah Road just west of the Canoochee River. There is, however, no definitive information on when it terminated operation. It appears that artisans manufactured the bricks used in most of the area antebellum houses at the building site. Workers mixed the clay, sand, and water together and then placed the material in molds. The mason or brick maker then stacked the "green" bricks in a temporary kiln and fired them to hardness. Masons mixed mortar by combining lime with sand and water. Their work included constructing brick chimneys and foundation piers.[32]

One trade not represented in the area was plastering. Although many of the houses in more populated sections used plaster to cover interior walls, this material was apparently considered an unnecessary luxury in the area of

Figure 2.3
(A) Tattnall County farmer and politician Benjamin Brewton operated the second Brewton Mill on Cedar Creek. His father, Nathan Brewton, established the first mill at the mouth of Cedar Creek and the Canoochee River. Benjamin Brewton's mill included an "up-and-down" saw, a grist mill, and a cotton gin. *(B)* The millpond site. *(C)* Remnants of the mill are visible today.

A

B

C

study. Instead of plaster, planed heart pine planking was the material of choice for interior walls.

There were several types of doors utilized in the Evans County antebellum dwellings. They ranged from the large and intricately crafted four-panel doors in the A. D. Eason house to the plain batten type found in the Berry Brewton, Smith-Daniel, and Thomas A. Durrence houses. The batten door configuration consists of carefully fitted, wide vertical boards held together by chamfered, horizontal battens. The Edwards-Strickland house has at least one of the original doors that matched the other Federal-period details of the house. The locks for the doors include a wooden latch in the Smith-Daniel house and standard door surface mounted metal locks in the other houses. Doorknobs included examples of iron, brass, and porcelain manufacture.

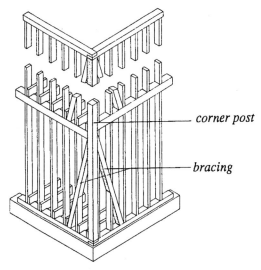

Figure 2.4
Braced-frame construction is prevalent in the nonlog houses of Evans County. (From *Old-House Dictionary*, by Steven J. Phillips. Reprinted by permission of John Wiley & Sons, Inc.)

The hall-and-parlor room arrangement was standard in the earlier dwellings, with the central hall occurring later in the antebellum period. The hall-and-parlor configuration normally had an enclosed staircase leading to the second floor from one of the two main rooms, whereas the central hall provided a more convenient location for the stairway. This arrangement allowed greater privacy for the rooms and gave a more stately interior appearance. It also provided a more symmetrical look to the exterior and interior.

Most area antebellum houses had detached kitchens (Fig. 2.5). The purpose of this arrangement was to prevent possible kitchen fires from spreading and to keep kitchen heat and noise away form the main house. Some kitchens had a pathway between the house and kitchen and others had a porch or breezeway connecting them. In later times, owners covered the porches for comfort and to keep the floor from deteriorating. The detached kitchen, often constructed first, became temporary quarters until completion of the main house.

In later years of the era, the houses often had ells added behind the main structure. These appendages often included a kitchen, dining room, and perhaps a bedroom. The porch area of an ell sometimes contained a well for convenience in drawing water.

In some cases the owner helped with the building process by procuring materials. For example, A. D. Eason in Undine provided most of the lumber, hardware, and paint for his house. The main building material, longleaf yellow heart pine, was available in large quantities in the region. Other items, however, such as glass, nails, hardware, and paint were generally expensive since they had to be ordered from Savannah or elsewhere.

The antebellum plantations in Tattnall and Bulloch counties were self-sufficient entities. The plantation contained a complex of outbuildings including kitchens, smokehouses, boiler houses, barns, sugarhouses, cotton houses, and slave houses. Most of these support buildings were for food production, preservation, or storage. Normally located several miles apart, the plantations became their own complete communities.

Original owners of seven of the nine houses in the survey had nearby family cemeteries. The only exceptions were the John Rogers and Thomas Rogers families who utilized the Bull Creek Baptist Church cemetery located within two miles of their houses.

Owners built most of the antebellum houses in this survey in the 1850s. It is safe to characterize the building process for these dwellings as traditional and labor-intensive. In this rural area, the older braced-frame construction and site-fired bricks were standard. There is no evidence of architect-designed houses. Rather, the house's plan seemed to evolve from a close collaboration between the owner and local carpenter. The plantation owners were very self-sufficient and actively participated in the building process by supplying materials, tools, and labor.

THE EVOLUTION OF THE PLAIN PLANTATION HOUSE
Figure 2.5

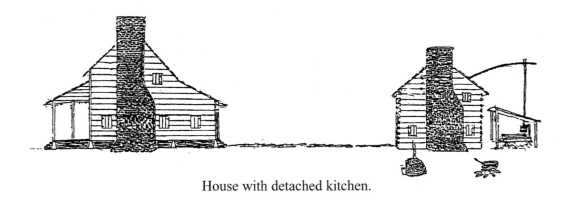

House with detached kitchen.

Covered porch connecting house and kitchen.

Plantation Plain house with rear ell.

(Drawings by Rita Turner Wall from
"Genesis of the Southern Plantation House")

Figure 3.1
The A.D. Eason House in 1998.

3   A. D. EASON HOUSE

Abraham Darlington Eason (1816-1887) was the youngest son of pioneer Methodist minister William Eason and his wife, Sarah. William Eason came to Tattnall County from Colleton County, South Carolina, and preached his first sermon in his new county of residence in 1802. William Eason later founded Mt. Carmel, the first Methodist church in Tattnall County. Prior to his death in 1831, William Eason was active as a preacher and in the religious life of the area.[1]

Abraham grew up in the Mt. Carmel community located four miles northeast of Reidsville. In 1843 he married Susan Tillman (1827-1907), the daughter of Joseph and Catherine Tillman. Joseph was a planter and large landowner who lived near his ferry operation on the Canoochee River. Abraham and Susan moved to nearby Dry Creek in 1844 and built a log home there in what is now the community of Undine in Evans County.[2]

A. D. Eason House Floor Plan

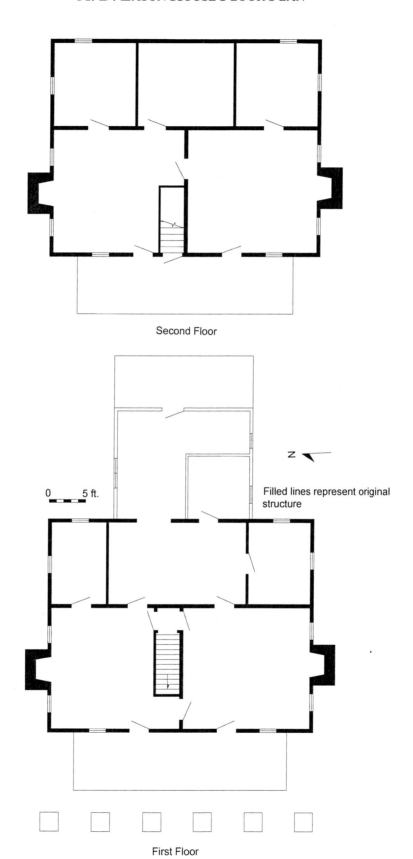

Second Floor

0 _ _ 5 ft.

Filled lines represent original structure

First Floor

Abraham, active in the affairs of his community, served Tattnall County in several positions including Georgia General assembly representative, justice of the inferior court, and tax receiver and collector. He was one of the organizing trustees of the Tattnall County Methodist Campground.[3]

By 1850 Abraham had accumulated more than 5,500 acres through state grants and purchases. In addition to operating his plantation, he was also a surveyor. He purchased 5,157 acres of the estate land of his deceased father-in-law, Joseph Tillman, in 1851. Among the parcels in this estate was one originally granted to Moses Jernigan for 700 acres on Dry Creek and the Canoochee River. It was upon this land that Abraham built the log home that he replaced a few years later with one of the county's most prominent homes.[4]

Abraham Eason was a man of great industry. He kept meticulous records of his surveying and farming enterprises. As time went on, his business prospered and his family grew. By 1854 he began acquiring materials to build a fine new house. He hired a local carpenter, Amos Hearn (Fig. 3.2B), to build the dwelling. Hearn began the project in July of 1856.[5]

Abraham kept an account book in which he detailed the construction expenses for the house. As a result we have one of the most complete accounts of mid-1850s building costs and practices for any antebellum house in the area. Eason chronicled such events as his family's first meal in the dining room and the date they initially built fires in the fireplaces.[6]

It took Amos Hearn a little over eleven months to build the house, and the Easons moved in one year to the day from the date Hearn began construction. They first moved into the detached kitchen and later into the house.[7]

A. D. Eason's Account Book[8]

Abraham Eason was an well-organized person. During his lifetime he kept a series of account books (Fig. 3.4A), several of which exist today. Carefully preserved by the Eason family since the 1850s, these diary-like books are small enough to fit in a shirt pocket. No doubt Eason frequently carried them with him. Some of the books contain field notes from his surveys, and others provide details of the operation of his substantial plantation.

Fortunately, one of these small volumes includes information about construction of his house. Begun in July 1854, the book chronicles all labor and material costs. Moreover, it gives us much insight into building practices of the era.

The first item procured for the house construction was shingles. According to Eason, S. D. Vinson "commenced to getting shingles" in July 1854 and by September of that year Eason paid for them.

Hewing of the structural members was substantially complete by May of 1855, and Abraham paid for them in that month. It took Amos 24 days to assemble materials for the foundation, and he and other workers laid it on August 4. Prior to starting the framing of the house, Abraham accumulated other materials for construction including nails and a large order of wooden planking. Amos used the planks to construct the walls, ceilings, and floors. Although the account book does not give the location of the mill used to saw the planking, the Benjamin Brewton Mill on Cedar Creek was less than five miles away.

The house "raising" occurred on the 20th and 21st of August in 1856. No doubt Abraham's neighbors assisted in this labor-intensive task. This event usually included a great feast and community social at its conclusion.

As was often the practice, the mason built the chimneys after workers substantially completed the house. According to Abraham's records, Hugh Casady "commenced laying brick" for the chimney in January 6, 1858. The 1860 census for Bulloch County lists Casady as a master mason born in Scotland. His double-shoulder chimneys had fireplaces on both floors. An account entry of January 14, indicates the family "built fires in the 2 fireplaces in the south east chimney." The exact length of time it took to build the other chimney is unknown, but Abraham paid Casady's bill in April.

The book also details the payment for lime to make the brick mortar used for the chimneys. In December of 1857, Abraham paid S. D. Vinson for making the bricks that were apparently fired on site in a temporary kiln.

The account book also lists the hardware purchased for the house. It includes butt hinges, screws, locks, clothes hooks, and fasteners for the wooden blinds. The doors have handsome, marbleized porcelain knobs. The original clothes hooks remain in the left rear room downstairs.

Abraham detailed costs to paint the house including bills for pigment, oil, and lead. Other painting materials purchased include buckets and brushes. The Eason family still has one of these buckets and brushes (Fig. 3.10*E*) used to paint the house, and hardened paint remains in the bottom of the bucket. They found these relics in the attic along with nails and other materials used in the house's construction. Abraham lists payments to Alfred Montgomery and Amos Hearn for painting the house.

The total cost of the house, including materials and labor, was $1,904.67. Further displaying his acumen for business, Abraham had each of the three principal workers at the house, Hearn, Casady, and Vinson sign the account book stating that they received full payment.

Not only did Hearn sign the account book, he also left his autograph in chalk on a rafter brace in the attic of the house (Fig. 3.10*A*). A neighbor, Sol Kennedy, did likewise and apparently assisted in building the dwelling. No doubt their bold signatures indicated their pride in building one of the finest houses in the county.

HOUSE SURVEY

The Eason house is a two-story double-pile, or full two-room deep structure. As a result it is larger than the Plantation Plain dwellings found elsewhere in the county. The highly finished interior trim of the house shows Greek Revival influence in boldness and proportion (Fig. 3.8). The ceiling molding, fireplace mantel, window surrounds, chair rail with wainscoting, and doors all reflect similar style.

The house remains relatively unchanged with the exception of a later added kitchen. Fire destroyed the original detached kitchen that was behind the house.

The current owner of the house, Margaret Eason, and the late A. D. Eason, III, were married in 1939. Shortly after their marriage, they added a rear kitchen in the main part of the house. Previously there was a rear lean-to kitchen that, according to Margaret, fell into disrepair during the Depression of the 1930s. Margaret recalls that the old kitchen was so drafty, that she wore her coat while preparing meals for the family on cold winter days. She indicates the Rural Electrification Association wired the house for electricity in 1941.[9]

Margaret Eason replaced the chimneys in 1982 (Fig. 3.5A). That year also marked other remodeling including renovations to the bathroom and kitchen. Margaret also replaced the roof, the brick piers in front of the house, and rebuilt the chimneys and fireplaces to their original state (Fig. 3.7C). The front part of the house and the upstairs remain unaltered.[10]

The house has two front doors opening into the front rooms. A center wall, boxed stairway leads (Fig. 3.7B) from the front northside room to the outside, upper-story front porch, giving access to the upstairs rooms (Fig. 3.6C). This unusual feature allows increased usable square footage in the upstairs rooms. There are three doors on the upper front porch including one for the stairs and one for each of the two front rooms. The front porch area also has a highly finished appearance due to the planed, tongue-and-groove sheathing. The main rafters in the roof extend to the front edge of the porch providing a continuous roofline, as opposed to the other antebellum houses of the county where the front porch takes the form of an appendage.

The house's 11" by 11" hand-hewn foundation sills rest on brick piers. A notable feature on the front porch and throughout the interior of the house is the heart pine planking. These boards range in width from 9" to 13" and are virtually knot-free.

The dominant feature of the house is the double gallery or two-story front porch and six cased, free standing 21' 10" square columns set on brick piers (Fig. 3.6B) The columns with their plain capitals (Fig. 3.5B) provides a hint of the Doric order. Indicative of Greek Revival style, the columns create an imposing facade. Seating of the columns on brick bases adds enhanced proportions to the house. Additionally, this feature retards rotting of the porch floor because water drips from the roof onto the ground and brick piers rather than onto the wooden porch. The lower porch has columns supporting the upper gallery. Wooden rails enclose the porches on both stories.

If there is a rare jewel in the crown of Evans County antebellum architecture, the A. D. Eason house is it. The house, perfectly sited on a slight knoll, looks as if it grew out the ground instead of being built. It has the appearance that it has always been there, and Evans County's architectural legacy would not be as rich without this exquisite example of antebellum building. The Eason family treasures the house and the artifacts that document its construction (Fig. 3.4). This family sets a fine example in preserving architectural history for future generations.

July 3rd 1854 S. D. Vinson commenced getting shingles

July 8th 1856 A. J. Hearn commenced building the house

August 4th 1856 Laid the foundation

August 20th and 21st Raised the house

First bill of plank, 130.00
2nd bill of plank,   <u>151.13</u>
altogether   281.13
3rd bill of plank,   <u>23.28</u>
                    304.91

June 1st 1857 Montgomery commenced painting

Due at the mill for $23.75

June the 25th 1857 Hearn finished all but putting in the sash and a lock to one door

July the 8th 1857 Moved in to the new house

J. A. Futch left hear [here] the 3rd day of July 1857

July 28th 1857 A. J. Hearn finished the wood work of the house

January 6th 1858 Hugh Casady commenced laying brick

Expenses		$	cts
May 1855			
	paid for plank	156	00
September 1854			
	paid for shingles	42	00
May 1856			
	paid for huegin [hewing]	18	00
June 1856			
	paid for nails	24	75

August 1856

        paid for nails   1   00

October 1st 1856

paid for nails	4	50
paid for sash	39	96
paid for blinds	50	60
paid for sash locks	1	25
paid for but [butt] hinges	7	36
paid for screws	3	60
paid for blind fastenings	3	12
paid for paint	26	15
paid for locks	14	40
paid for oil	10	80
paid for cans	1	80
paid for brushes	2	08
paid for led [lead]	6	90
paid for one pair blinds	2	25

April 16th 1857

paid for locks	1	00
paid for scotching	1	87
paid for nails	1	00

April 25th 1857

paid for plank	133	10

May 12th 1857

paid for close [clothes] hooks	3	00
paid for screws		37

May 19th 1857

paid for lyme [lime]	3	50

May 26th 1857

paid for nails	12	50

June 6th 1857

paid Cassedy for laying brick	6	30

June 10th

paid for springs		12½
paid for oil	18	12½
paid for one lock	1	25
paid for paint	30	31

June 25th 1857

paid A. J. Hearn for building	805	50
paid A. J. Hearn for painting	3	00
paid for paint	2	66

July 23rd 1857

paid for paint and oil	6	00

August 7th

paid Alford Montgomery	83	00

December 1857

paid James Martin for making brick	27	06

December 23rd

Paid for lyme [lime]	4	00

April 10th 1858

paid Hue Cassedy	65	00

Georgia, Tattnall County. Received of A. D. Eason eight hundred and fourteen dollars and 50/100 in full satisfaction of all demands up to this day the 25th of June 1857.

A. J. Hearn

Georgia, Tattnall County. Received of A. D. Eason sixty five dollars in full of all demands for building two brick chimneys and piers under the house. This 10th day of April 1858.

Hugh Cassedy

Georgia, Tattnall County. Received of A. D. Eason eighty five dollars in full of all demand for painting a house. This 7th day of Aug 1857.

Alfred Montgomery

February 14th 1844 moved to Dry Creek

January 29th 1857 moved from the old house into the new ketching [kitchen]

May 30th 1857 eat dinner in the new dining room

July the 8th 1857 Moved in to the new house

January 14th 1858 built fires in the 2 fireplaces in the south east chimney

A

B

Figure 3.2
(*A*) Abraham D. Eason. (Photo courtesy
of Margaret Eason) *(B)* Amos J. Hearn,
builder. (Photo courtesy of Emily
Groover.)

Figure 3.3
Deerskin-covered
bible used by A. D.
Eason's father,
pioneer minister
William Eason.
(Photo courtesy of
Margaret Eason)

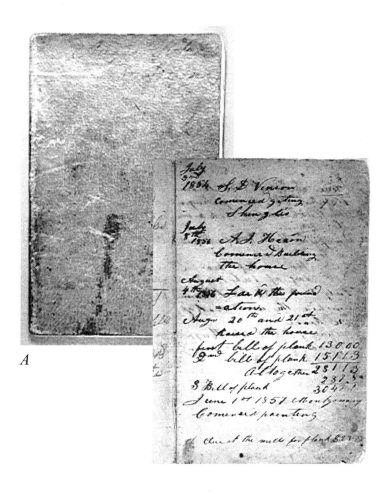

A

B

C

Figure 3.4
(A) Abraham D. Eason kept meticulous records of building expenses in his account book. The Eason family carefully preserved these historic documents through the years. *(B)* Copy of an original state land grant to A. D. Eason. *(C)* Copy of original plat for land where Eason constructed his home. (All documents on this page courtesy of Margaret Eason)

Figure 3.5
(A) Double-shouldered chimneys are at both gable ends of the house. *(B)* Molding trim adds simple elegance to front porch column capital.

A

B

A

Figure 3.6
(A) Second floor porch. *(B)* Double-galleried porch and columns provide Greek Revival embellishments. *(C)* The upstairs porch has two front doors leading into the rooms and one door heading the staircase. This unique feature provides more usable interior space. *(D)* Marbleized porcelain doorknobs.

B

C

D

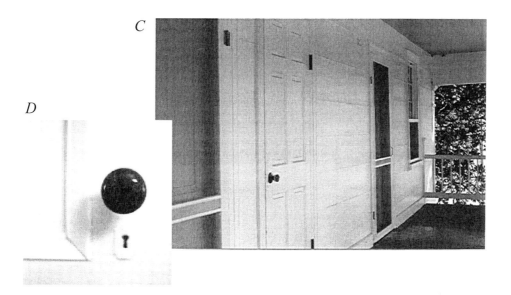

A

B

Figure 3.7
(A) Heart pine flooring in the upstairs rooms has rare gnarled pattern.
(B) Stairs leading to the front porch on second floor. *(C)* Fireplace with Greek Revival mantle trim.

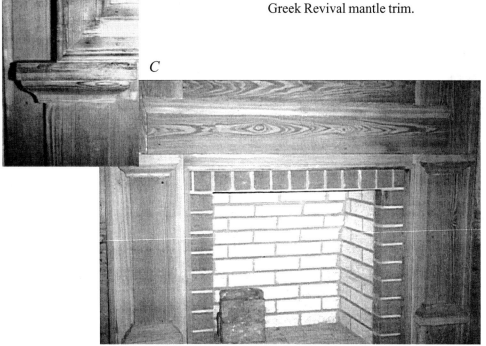

C

HOUSES OF HEART PINE

A

C

Figure 3.8
(A) Upstairs door separating two front rooms. (B) 13" planks in upstairs bedroom. (C) Finely crafted door and matching chair rail in downstairs room.

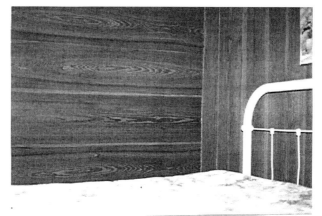

B

A

Figure 3.9
(A) Family antiques add to
interior charm of the house.
(B) Dining table made from
leftover wood from the house
construction.

B

HOUSES OF HEART PINE

Figure 3.10
(A) The bold autograph of the house builder, Amos J. Hearn, is still visible in the attic. *(B)* Roof supports are joined by mortise-and-tenon joints. *(C)* Handmade brick from original chimney. *(D)* Heart pine wooden peg measures 1" thick by 7" long. *(E)* Original paint bucket and brushes used for painting the house. *(F)* Metal wedge used in construction of the house.

Figure 3.11
Saddle-jointed log corncrib located
on house grounds.

Figure 3.12
Eason House
in 1954. (Photo
courtesy of
Margaret Eason)

Figure 4.1
The Berry Brewton House.

4   BERRY BREWTON HOUSE

One of the two antebellum houses in Bellville is the Benjamin "Berry" Brewton House. Located on the eastern edge of the town north of Highway 280 on the land of Warren Wilbanks, the house stands about 100 yards east of its original site. Wilbanks moved the house to its present location shortly after he bought it and the surrounding acreage in 1959 from Berry Brewton's youngest son, Theodore.[1]

Benjamin Berrian "Berry" Brewton (1834-1911) was the son of Tattnall County farmer and politician Benjamin Brewton and his wife, Charlotte. Berry's grandparents were Nathan and Nancy Brewton and Jonathan and Eliza Bacon.[2]

In 1860, Berry Brewton bought 393½ acres from his future brother-in-law, William E. Tippins. The parcel was a combination of state land grants to Charles B. Mulford in 1814 and William Hodges in 1836. Tippins's land

BERRY BREWTON HOUSE FLOOR PLAN

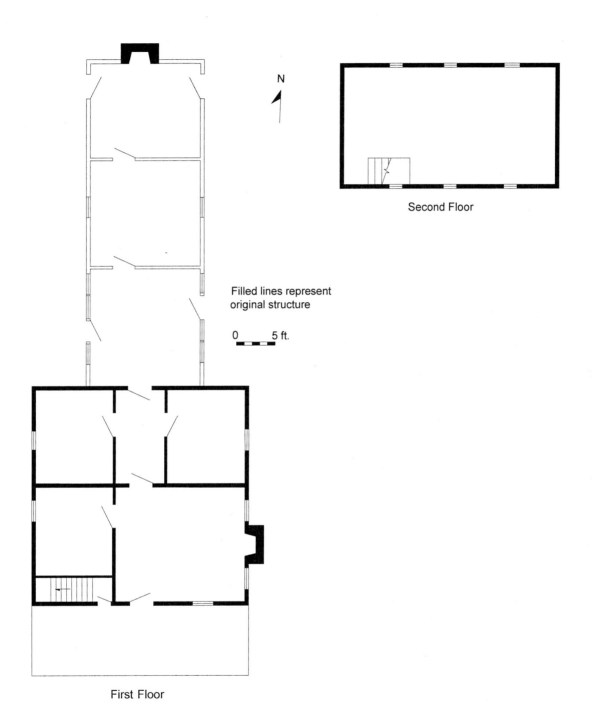

N

Second Floor

Filled lines represent
original structure

0 _____ 5 ft.

First Floor

included a house that, according to Evans County historian Theodore Brewton, dates to 1856. A storm blew down the original structure, and Tippins rebuilt it in 1857 or 1858.[3]

William Tippins had the lumber used for the house sawn at the Benjamin Brewton Mill on Cedar Creek. This mill, about two miles east of the house, employed an old "up-and-down" reciprocating saw powered by water from a millpond on the creek. The mill belonged to Berry's father, whose home was nearby. Berry worked at the mill as a young boy.[4]

Berry married Candace Tippins, daughter of William and Mary Tippins, in 1863. A member of the 61st Georgia Regiment, Berry was on furlough from the Confederate Army at the time. He participated in most of the major engagements of the Army of Northern Virginia and was wounded at the battle of Gettysburg. After his capture in September 1864, he spent time in a Union prison camp at Pt. Lookout, Maryland.[5]

Later in the war, conditions were difficult as Candace tried to manage the farm. In an 1864 letter from Virginia, Berry expressed his concern when he advised Candace to only "tend the best of the up land" and not to be overly ambitious with her farm work. Despite her difficulties, Candace was able to maintain the house and farm during her husband's absence.[6]

After the war, Berry returned to farming and involvement in the timber trade. He owned a large tract of land in the present-day town of Bellville, and sold many of the building lots to early community settlers. He was also instrumental in the establishment of the Bellville Academy and the Bellville Methodist Church.[7]

Berry died in 1911 and Candace the following year.

HOUSE SURVEY

Theodore Brewton inherited his father's home place and lived there until he sold the property to Warren Wilbanks. After Wilbanks purchased the house, he hired Wesley Bashlor from Pembroke to separate the main house from the attached kitchen. Bashlor then moved the structures to their present locations. The house previously faced south, but Bashlor reoriented it to the north. He reused the house's brick piers at the new site. The kitchen became part of a storage shed located just north of the house (Fig. 4.7).[8]

At the time of Wilbanks's purchase, there was no running water in the house and only rudimentary electrical service. According to Wilbanks, there was a large fireplace on the east end of the house. The handmade brick chimney's fireplace was wide enough for cooking.[9]

One of the two original wells is still present on the south side of Wilbanks's home (Fig. 4.6A). Between this well and the house was a branch of the old Savannah Road. According to Theodore Brewton, Theodore's father welcomed people to stop for conversation, water, and rest. A horse lot was just south of the well, and travelers used this location to water and feed their horses.[10]

The one-and-a-half-story house is a variation of the Plantation Plain form. It has a full-width front porch and back lean-to rooms. The upstairs configuration, however, is one large room. Wilbanks hired Aubrey Glisson to add the wings to the east and west sides during a renovation shortly after moving the house. Several years later, Wilbanks found split rails in the woods near the site and used them to reconstruct the fence (Fig. 4.6C).[11]

Wilbanks relates that when he purchased the home, it had a picket fence in front. Vintage photos reveal the front porch posts rested on brick piers. There was a corncrib on the south side of the well and other small farm buildings on the property. Candace Brewton planted the crepe myrtle and cedar trees that still thrive at the house site.[12]

The original portion of the house is relatively unaltered. The ceiling, walls, and floors are heart pine planks (Fig. 4.4). The foundation sills are hand-hewn 8" by 8" timbers, and the construction method is braced-frame. The 7' high rooms have simple wainscoting created by horizontal boards to a height of 32". A 4" molded chair rail separates these boards from the top vertical boards (Fig. 4.4A). Heart pine batten doors perfectly match the other woodwork of the handsome interior (Fig. 4.5B). The house construction shows superior workmanship, and the wood is of excellent quality.

The upstairs floor consists of one room. The ceiling of the room is 7' 10" in the center and tapers down with the roofline. The facade has three small one-over-one windows equally spaced between the top of the porch roof and main roof. The Brewtons used this room as a dormitory for the children. An interesting feature of the stairs is that they originally opened to an outside door. According to Wilbanks, this arrangement was to provide the children access to the upper floor without having to go through the main part of the house.[13]

The Berry Brewton House, one of the smaller Plantation Plain antebellum dwellings in Evans County, must be seen on the inside to fully appreciate its charm. While it is of modest size, its plain, heart pine interior is one of the most attractive examined during the county survey. The house provides a good example of the home of a yeoman farmer and his family.

Figure 4.2
Berry Brewton was a member of Company B of the 61st Georgia
Infantry. He married Candace Tippins in 1863 while on leave from the
army.

Figure 4.3
The Berry
Brewton House
circa 1950.
(Photo courtesy
of Ray DeLoach.)

A

B

Figure 4.4
(A) Vertical and horizontal heart pine planks form the interior walls. Note chair rail. *(B)* Batten doors with brass knobs. *(C)* Uncased stairs lead to a single room on second floor.

C

A

B

Figure 4.5
(A) House hardware. *(B)* Batten door. *(C)* Heart pine planks in ceiling of front porch.

C

A

Figure 4.6
(A) Original well south of the former house site.
(B) One of the handmade bricks used in foundation piers of the house bears the paw prints of a cat. *(C)* Rail fence rebuilt by Warren Wilbanks.

B

C

Figure 4.7
Detail of clapboards covering
exterior of dining room/kitchen.
Formerly attached to the house by a
breezeway, the kitchen is now used
as a storage building.

Figure 5.1
The Brewton-Hendrix House in the 1940s. (Photo courtesy of Cleta McCorkle)

5   BREWTON-HENDRIX HOUSE

Jonathan Bacon Brewton (1827-1897) was the first-born child of Tattnall County farmer and politician Benjamin Brewton and wife, Charlotte. Jonathan's paternal grandparents, Nathan and Nancy Brewton, first came to the area from Warren County in 1794.[1]

Jonathan grew up near his father's mill on Cedar Creek, about one mile north of present-day Brewton Cemetery. He married Margaret Everett (1830-1919) of Bulloch County in 1848, and they established their home approximately one mile north of his father's mill on what is now Highway 129 North (Claxton-Metter Highway). Margaret was the daughter of John Carter Everett and his wife, Elizabeth Ellis Everett. Their marriage produced eleven children, including John Carter Brewton, cofounder and first president of Brewton-Parker College.[2]

In 1849 two of Jonathan's uncles, Samuel and Benjamin Brewton conveyed 300 acres on the Canoochee River to him for $600. Prior to Samuel

BREWTON-HENDRIX HOUSE FLOOR PLAN

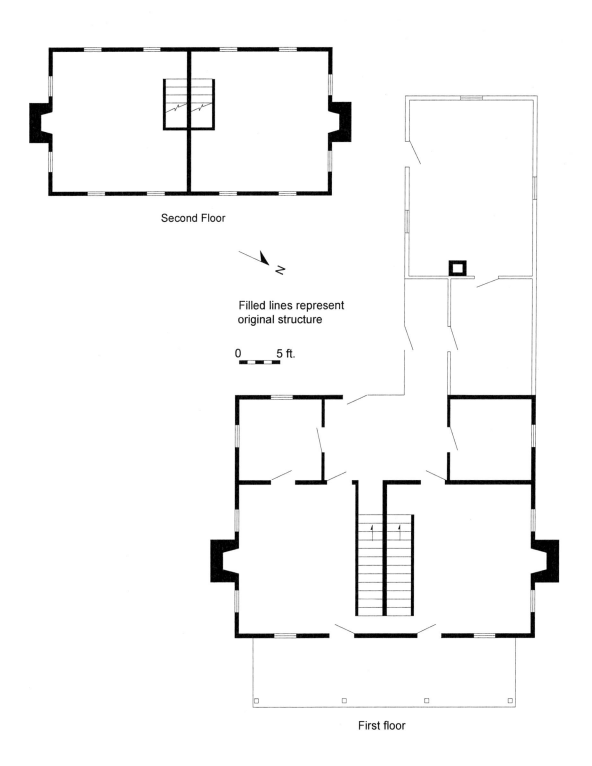

Second Floor

Filled lines represent
original structure

0   5 ft.

First floor

and Benjamin's ownership, the land was in the possession of yet another uncle, Nathan Brewton, Jr. Jonathan's grandfather, Nathan, Sr., was the original owner by virtue of a grant from the state. The northeast corner of this parcel was the site of Brewton Bridge on the Canoochee River. It is interesting to note, however, that the deed was executed in 1849, but not recorded until 1854. Apparently, his uncles held the deed until Jonathan finished payments on the land.[3]

The decade of the 1850s was significant for Jonathan Brewton and his family. He was administrator of his mother-in-law's estate, and he and his wife acquired land and slaves from this estate. Five of their 11 children were born between 1849 and 1859. Jonathan's wealth and the size of his family grew, thus providing both the means and need for a new house.

The 1860 census lists Jonathan as 33 years old, with 1,873 acres of real estate valued at $5,000. He had extensive livestock holdings and produced 200 bushels of corn during the previous year. His total evaluation was $11,200, with thirteen slaves and two slave houses. One of the slave houses remained until the 1950s.[4]

Jonathan served as Clerk of the Superior Court of Tattnall County and also represented the county for two terms in the Georgia House of Representatives. He served in the 5th Georgia Cavalry of the Confederate Army from late 1862 until February 1864, when residents elected him clerk of the court. In 1865 a foraging party from Sherman's invasion came through the eastern part of Tattnall County and stopped at the Brewton house. Jonathan fled to the Canoochee River swamps, and the Federals, knowing he was a county official, ransacked the house.[5]

Jonathan not only ran his farm, but also had other prosperous enterprises. He was owner of a general merchandise store located across the road from his residence. His other business interests included a gristmill, sawmill, and cotton gin. He operated a post office in his store, and this was also the site of a courthouse and voting precinct named Hawpond (Fig. 5.9). In 1888, the Shoals *Gazetteer of Georgia* lists Hawpond as having a population of 50. In later years, the building became a cotton storage house. It had a long porch and three doors on the front facade. In the early 1930s when the state paved the highway in front of the house, removal of the structure was necessary.[6]

The farm was the site of a brickmaking kiln in post-bellum years. Shortly after the turn of the twentieth century, the Register and Glennville Railroad was laid through the Brewton farm.[7]

Local tradition holds that the home was a stage stop on a branch of the Old Sunbury Road passing in front. This 1790s road led from Sunbury in Liberty County to Greensboro in Washington County and skirted between watercourses for most of its length. Known for his hospitality, Brewton maintained a well with a sweep to assist travelers in obtaining water. The configuration of the house with its separated upstairs bedrooms was also conducive to accommodating overnight travelers.[8]

Several old-time area residents assert that Amos J. Hearn, who also constructed the A. D. Eason home in Undine, built the Brewton home. Located about two miles apart, there are several very similar details of the two houses. Among the common traits are the two front doors, top molding details on the front porch columns, porch rail details, and pattern of wainscoting in the front rooms. Though tax records indicate a likely construction date of 1858, the exact date of construction is difficult to pinpoint.[9]

House Survey

The Jonathan Brewton house is a classic 1850s Plantation Plain structure. Its two front doors lead into hall-and-parlor rooms. It originally had twin, separated stairs leading to the second-floor rooms (Fig. 5.7). The upstairs center wall kept the boys and girls separated and also made it easier to accommodate travelers on the stage route. According to one former resident of the house, the upstairs partition was not completely effective in maintaining separation. The children of the house often playfully went out of one upstairs window onto the porch roof and into a window on the other side.[10]

The front porch has cased columns with simple, molded capitals (Fig. 5.3A). The square balustrade porch railing is mortise-and-tenon construction. Horizontal planks cover the exterior wall under the porch. Other features of the house included vertical solid wood shutters; wood shingled roof; exterior weatherboards; brick piers supporting the foundation; and two exterior-end "double shoulder," corbel-capped chimneys. Vintage photographs show the presence of six-over-six pane windows (Fig. 5.2B).

The front rooms have beaded heart pine planking. They have wainscoting consisting of horizontal boards below the chair rail and vertical boards above. Wooden planks with simple molding form the ceiling. The floors are made of tongue-and-groove heart pine boards (Fig. 5.3D). The foundation sills are 11" by 11" hand-hewn timbers (Fig. 5.3C).

The house has a later-added rear ell (Fig. 5.4). It appears that the kitchen/dining room was originally detached and subsequently connected to the rest of the house by a porch. The porch, at one time open, is now enclosed. The appendage contains the kitchen, dining room, and a bedroom. The original chimney in this part of the house served both a cook stove in the kitchen and fireplace in the dining room.[11]

The farmstead had the usual outbuildings including boiler shelter, smoke house (Fig. 5.10), cotton house, and barns. The dwelling had big magnolia trees on each side, as well as a picket fence in front. Cedar trees once lined the roads in front and on the side of the house.[12]

After Jonathan died in 1897, his widow acquired the house and surrounding 377 acres as dower rights. She continued to live there until 1902 or 1903 when she moved to Hagan. In 1910, her youngest son, Henry J. Brewton acquired the house and land. He retained it until debt default resulted in Union Central Life Insurance Company taking title. The company sold the house to James A. Hendrix in 1936. Hendrix had previously lived in the home and sharecropped the land for a number of years. Members of the Hendrix family owned the house until 1990 when they sold it to the present owners, Susan and George Willcox.[13]

Cleta McCorkle, a daughter of Jim Hendrix, returned in 1978 to live in her childhood home. She remodeled the dwelling shortly thereafter. Among the changes were new windows and insulation downstairs; removal of one of the two stairways; elimination of the second floor separating wall; installation of a bathroom upstairs and in the downstairs rear bedroom; installation of closets upstairs; elimination of pantry areas in the kitchen; and enlargement of the opening from the front north room to the back shed portion of the house. McCorkle's contractor, Austin Lewis, also removed the old chimneys and rebuilt the one on the north end. Except for the removal of the chimneys, much of the outside of the main house remains original.[14]

Two blanket chests used in the house remain with Brewton family descendants (Fig. 5.8). One was reportedly made from heart pine left over from the house's construction and the other was used for tool storage during the building of the house.[15]

The Jonathan Brewton House remains one of the county's best examples of Plantation Plain architecture. The house still retains its basic character and is largely original in its exterior. Its commanding facade and interesting history make it a landmark in the rural Evans County landscape.

A

B

Figure 5.2
(A) Jonathan B. and Margaret Brewton. *(B)* Early 1900s photo of Brewton-Hendrix House shows window shutters and lineup of left front door with the back door. (All photos on this page courtesy of John Rabun, Jr.)

A

B

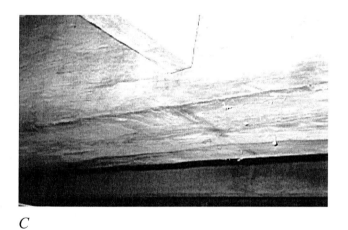

C

Figure 5.3
(A) Detail of front porch column capital. *(B)* Vintage photo of south elevation shows double-shouldered chimney and kitchen in the rear. *(C)* 11" by 11" sills provide a solid foundation. *(D)* Heart pine flooring is present throughout the house.

D

Figure 5.4
1970 views of the house.
(Photos courtesy of John
Rabun, Jr.)

Figure 5.5
Brewton-Hendrix House in 1998.

A   B

Figure 5.6
Local carpenter Amos Hearn built the Jonathan Brewton
House and the nearby A. D. Eason House. Several archi-
tectural details of the houses are very similar. (*A*) Engaged
porch rail on Brewton House and (*B*) same element on the
A. D. Eason House.

Figure 5.7
Original house configuration included two stair-
cases – one on either side of the wall between the
two front rooms. These stairs led to separated
boys' and girls' bedrooms on the floor above.

Figure 5.8
Wooden box used for
tool storage during
construction of
house is now used as
a blanket chest.

Figure 5.9
Jonathan Brewton's general store also served as the Hawpond
community courthouse. (From *A History of Our Locale*.)

Figure 5.10
Brewton farm smokehouse stands on the south side of the main house.

Figure 6.1
The Simon J. Brewton House in 1993.

6   SIMON J. BREWTON HOUSE

Simon J. Brewton (1819-1865) was the youngest child of Tattnall and Bulloch county pioneers Nathan and Nancy Brewton. Nathan bought his first land in the area in 1794 and became one of the section's largest property owners by acquiring over 9,500 acres in grants from the state and by purchase. Simon established his home north of the Canoochee River, and the structure is the only existing antebellum house in the part of Evans County that was formerly Bulloch. The property on which Simon built his home was a gift from his father in 1843. The structure is three miles north of Claxton on the east side of Highway 301.[1]

      Simon was a farmer, large property owner, and very active politician. In January of 1861 the residents of Bulloch County elected him Justice of the Inferior Court, and he held that office until January 1865. They also chose him to attend the October 1865 Georgia Constitutional Convention in

Simon Brewton House Floor Plan

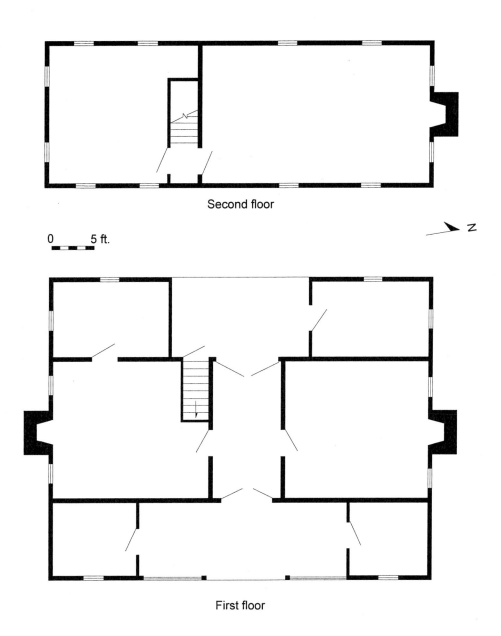

Second floor

0 ___ 5 ft.

N

First floor

Milledgeville. The *Savannah Daily News* of October 21, 1865, billed the convention as one that would decide the "political destiny and social and economic interests of our beloved state." The convention delegates wrote a new state constitution, annulled the Ordinance of Secession, and formally abolished slavery.[2]

The convention not only decided the destiny of Georgia, but unfortunately Simon's attendance also decided his. During his return from the state capital, he stayed overnight in a house where someone had smallpox. Stricken with the disease himself, he was deathly sick upon reaching home. Doctors Seaborn Hodges and James Lewis attended Simon, but were unable to save his life. Other members of the household contracted the disease but recovered. The probate records of Bulloch County contain Dr. Lewis's $100 invoice for "medicine and direction" in treating Simon and his family.[3]

Simon married twice. He wed Matilda Tippins (1823-1861) in 1843, and after her death, he married her sister, Parthenia (1837-1898), in 1862. Simon and his wives had eleven children. After Simon's death, Parthenia took her dower rights in the house and surrounding 782-acre tract.[4]

Subsequent to his marriage in March 1843, Simon received property from his father the following September, and later built his house on this parcel. However, it was apparently a number of years before he built his own dwelling, as the 1850 Bulloch County census shows Simon and his family still living in his parents' household. Nathan died in 1855 and his widow, Nancy, moved in with Simon in 1859. She lived with Simon and his family until shortly before her death in 1864.[5]

With the provision that Parthenia retain dower rights in the property, she sold the house and land to her sons Henry C. and William F. Brewton in 1875. The heirs of William F. Brewton acquired the property in 1894 and sold it to William H. Brewton in 1902. William H. owned the house and surrounding 670 acres from 1902 until 1925 when Floyd Baggett acquired the parcel. Baggett was the husband of Edna Brewton, a daughter of William H. Brewton. Baggett moved the Brewton house to its current location in the early 1950s, and he then built a brick home on the old site. Cynthia Henry, a granddaughter of Floyd Baggett, now owns the house and surrounding acreage.[6]

The original form of the house is Plantation Plain with central hall. The main part of the dwelling is the largest found in the county survey. It also is the only house in the survey that has rooms on either end of both the front porch and back lean-to portion of the structure. The house also had a separate kitchen attached via a breezeway porch. The tenons on the breezeway sill are still visible (Fig. 6.5A). The expert workmanship evident in the house indicates the skill of the builder. House construction techniques, deeds, and census data place the construction date in the early 1850s.[7]

It is likely that Simon and his slaves participated in the building of the house. After Simon's death, the administrator of his estate sold four lots of carpenter's tools, kegs of nails, screws, paint, hinges, etc., in addition to the usual plantation tools (see page 82). Also included were a saw gin, timber cart, sawed lumber lots, cant hooks, crow bars, and a complete set of blacksmith tools. These items point to Simon's involvement in the timber and perhaps the building trades. A copy of the executor's estate appraisement is provided at the end of this chapter and gives much insight into the plantation tools and household furnishings of the period.[8]

The Simon Brewton house is now used as a barn. The underlying structure of the dwelling, however, is still intact (Fig. 6.6). Originally the location of the home was approximately 500 yards north on present-day Highway 301 at the site of the Baggett house. An old well used by the Brewton family is still at the original house location. Even though it is regrettable that the building is no longer used as a home, its current configuration provides an excellent opportunity to clearly view the original structural timbers.

The house construction is heart pine throughout. When the owners converted it to a barn, they covered the exterior with galvanized tin. Other modifications included removal of the two exterior-end chimneys, placing the house on a concrete block foundation, and removing other internal structural elements. The block foundation extends to the barn addition on the east side of the structure. Another change was the eastern reorientation for the front of the house. The part of the dwelling visible to the west on Highway 301 is the original back of the house.[9]

The joinery in this house reflects sophisticated building techniques. The main internal vertical structural members by the hall exterior doorways have a "T" shape and are hand-hewn 11" by 11" timbers (Fig. 6.4). These uniquely shaped heart pine supports go from the ground floor through the second floor to the ceiling as one continuous, 16' 9" support post. Mortise-and-tenon joints are present throughout the structure, and wooden pegs secure the joints. The blind mortise joints have notching that further aids structural integrity and indicates the expertise of the builder.

Four-by-four-inch diagonal downbraces support the corners of the structure, giving strength to the corner posts (Fig. 6.3). The walls, ceiling, and floors are planed planks ranging in size from 4" to 13" wide and fit together with tongue-and-groove joints. In addition to the wooden pegs and pins used to secure the structural joints, builders used flathead cut nails on the planking.

The roof system is not original. The rafter joints are not mortised nor does the wood match that used in other parts of the house. The roof pediment on what is now the west side of the house is a later addition, which was apparently incorporated to update the appearance of the house.

The house has window shutters on both stories (Fig. 6.2A). The downstairs windows had glazing, whereas the upstairs windows did not. The most interesting components of the house's little remaining hardware are the door and window shutter hinges. The hinges are made of forged cast iron, and flathead screws fasten them to the wood casements (Fig. 6.2B). Those that remain intact still work perfectly.

There are several generations of paint present in the house. The two front porch and two back shed rooms are silver-gray. Red spray paint covers the west side exterior of the structure.

The stairs to the upper floor no longer exist; however, there is clear evidence of their original configuration. They began on the back porch area and went up in the direction of the front of the house. The landing at the top of the stairs provided an entrance to either of the second-floor rooms. The family used the smaller of these rooms as a bedroom. The Brewtons used the other one for weaving, sewing, and a craft area for home manufacturing. The weaving room was large and included an exterior-end fireplace in a common chimney with the fireplace on the lower floor. The weaving room was apparently the site of considerable activity as there were up to three spinning wheels in operation in the house.[10]

As a result of the second-floor room configuration, the builder made the upstairs window placement asymmetrical. Both front and back elevations have four windows upstairs. However, the windows are not equidistant as seen in the other Plantation Plain houses in the county. Apparently the need for dispersed lighting and improved ventilation in the large upper story room outweighed the owner's desire for symmetry.

The Simon Brewton House at one time was a very grand dwelling for the area. Its large floor plan of eight rooms in the main section of the house, unusually shaped "T" support columns, and asymmetrical window arrangement give it features not present in any of the other extant antebellum buildings. Though no longer usable as a house, its remaining patterns, materials, and form give us a glimpse of its former functionality and attractiveness.

Inventory and Appraisement of the Estate of S. J. Brewton, Deceased[11]

1 Black mare	$150	63 lbs bacon	
1 Bay mare	150	- .20 pr lb	126.40
1 Sorrel Colt	50	1 1/2 bbls sugar	30
1 Mule - Bick	150	1 1/2 bbls syrup	25
1 Mule - Kate	150	1 Tub lard	15
2 Yoke oxen	100	1 Bank seed potatoes	15
80 Head cattle		1 Steel trap	.30
- $10 per head	800	2 Bells	2
65 Head hogs		1 Lot of plow gear	5
- $3 pr head	195	Saddles, bridles	
100 Head sheep		& sheep skins	15
- $2 pr head	250	1 Lot old buggy harness	3
10,135 lbs seed cotton		1 Lot plow stock &c	8
- 12 1/2 cts pr.	1266.87	1 Wagon cover	.50
1 Saw gin & gear	125	1 Set wagon wheels	50
1 Timber cart	35	1 Lot cow hides	13.75
1 Horse cart	30	1 Lot tanned leather	30
1 Ox cart	30	1 Lot rough rice	15
1 Buggy	50	1 Fish net	10
1 Rockaway	50	1 Lot cotton bagging	8
1 Set black smith tools	40	1 Lot kegs & nails	3
1 lot old iron	10	1 Lot ropes	10
1 Lot carpenters tools	50	1 Box & contents	3
1 Lot lumber	2	1 Pair steelyards	1.50
2 Scything cradles	10	1 Pair sheep shears	1.50
2 Grind stones	5	1 Crow bar	1.50
10 Bee hives	20	2 Slates & drow steelyards	1.50
1 Wheel barrow	1	115 Pieces of ranging timber	420
1 Buro	20	1 Lot fish hooks & line	1
1 Book case	8	Half interest in sugar mill	25
1 Lot books	20	4128 Acres of land	
1 Lounge	3	Bulloch County	6192
1 Clock	10	2010 Acres of land	
1 Double barrel gun	15	Tattnall County	2010
1 Rifle	15	297 Acres of land	
1 Chest	3	Emanuel County	297
1 Desk	16	1 Loom & gear	12
1 Table & glass	3	3 Spinning wheels	10
1 Wash stand	1.50	1 Sugar boiler & dipper	5
2 Pine boxes	1	Total	1583.84
1 Side board	4	Bank bills	827
1 Table	1.50	Amt. of Notes	1583
1 Lot shoe tools	5	Grand total	$15,663.66
1 Pr saddle bags	2		
5 Chairs	5		

(Note: Spelling and format as in original.; Bulloch County probate records, 1866, Simon J. Brewton.)

A

Figure 6.2
(A) Solid wooden shutters are present on both first- and second-floor windows. *(B)* Flathead screws hold shutter hinges in place. *(C)* Remnants of fireplace mantle.

B

C

A

B

Figure 6.3
(A) Mortise-and-tenon
joints secured with wooden
pegs provide corner
bracing. *(B)* Interior wall
brace.

Figure 6.4
Unique framing includes
"T" shaped hand-hewn
internal support posts.
Note porch rail in lower
left of photo.

A

B

Figure 6.5
(A) House sill at rear elevation shows mortise cavity that once held tenon connection. *(B)* View of sills from underneath the structure.

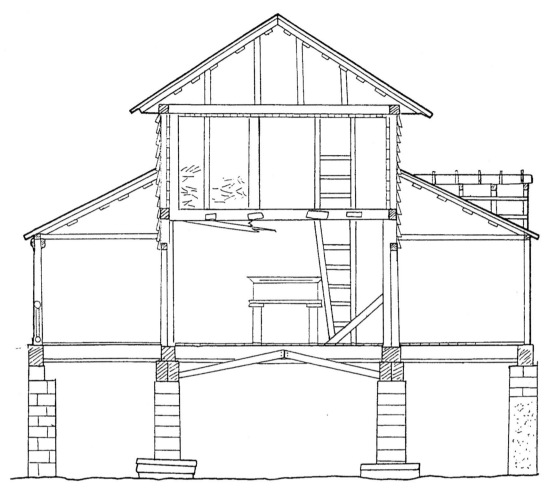

Figure 6.6
Brewton House north elevation profile showing
twentieth-century foundation modification for
conversion to barn. (Drawing from "Brewton
House-Claxton, Georgia" 1998 field survey by
Historic Preservation Department, Savannah College
of Art and Design)

Figure 6.7
Settlers' migration routes provided a diffusion path for
building ideas from state-to-state. Interestingly, this house,
found in Alabama, is almost identical to the configuration of
Evans County's Simon J. Brewton House. (Alabama
HABS photograph by W.N. Manning, 1935)

Figure 7.1
Herschel and Janie Durrence in front of their home in 1958. (Photo from Georgia Department of Archives and History Vanishing Georgia Collection)

7 THOMAS A. DURRENCE HOUSE

The Thomas A. Durrence home, located six miles south of Claxton and one-half mile east of Highway 301 on Tom McCall Road, is one of the county's largest Plantation Plain homes. Family tradition says the home's construction date was approximately 1858, the year Thomas (1831-1893) married Elizabeth Grice (1838-1922).[1]

Thomas was the son of Jesse A. Durrence (1784-1865) and Elizabeth Sands Durrence. Elizabeth Grice's parents were William and Evaline Smart Grice. Thomas and Elizabeth had nine children and 67 grandchildren.[2]

Thomas was a farmer, large landowner, public servant, and active participant in the religious life of the county. At the time of his death, his farm

Thomas A. Durrence House Floor Plan

Second Floor

N

Filled lines represent original structure

0   5 ft.

First Floor

comprised more than 2,700 acres. He represented Tattnall County in the Georgia General Assembly in 1886-7. Thomas and his wife were members of Brewton Methodist Church in what is now Hagan, and he served as a church trustee from 1859 until his death. He also served in the Georgia militia during the War Between the States.[3]

The 1860 agricultural census for Georgia lists Thomas as having 384 acres of land, 25 of which were improved. This property is also returned in the 1860 Tattnall County tax digest with a value of $800. There is no listing, however, for Thomas in the 1859 tax digest. This information would indicate he acquired his land sometime in late 1858 or 1859. The deed for this land acquisition was apparently not recorded.[4]

Thomas had the lumber for his home sawn at the Benjamin Brewton Mill on Cedar Creek. This old "up-and-down" mill sawed much of the timber used for area antebellum houses.[5]

After Thomas's death in 1893, his wife Elizabeth received the house and 64 acres of land as her dower. Elizabeth died in 1922. Their youngest son, Herschel Durrence, acquired title to the house in 1923 and lived there with his wife, Janie. She died in 1964 and he the following year. Tom McCall, a nephew of Herschel, inherited the house and resided there until his death in 1997. Debra Purcell, a granddaughter of Tom McCall, and husband Wayne Purcell now own the house.[6]

HOUSE SURVEY

The Plantation Plain house has a 7'10" wide central-hall with two first-floor and two second-floor rooms in the main part of the house and two rear-shed rooms joined by an open porch. From the rear-shed porch, the boxed, downstairs central-hall stairway (Fig. 7.6A) leads back-to-front to the upstairs hallway. Horizontal rails connected via newel posts surround two sides of the upper floor stair opening. The house's pressed tin roof rests on rafters nailed to a ridge board.[7]

The downstairs front rooms have wainscoting with horizontal planks on the walls above. The flooring, ceiling, and wall planks vary from 8" to 12" in width. Of particular note are the finely crafted metal hinges on the shutters (Fig. 7.8D). The locks on the interior doors carry a patent date of 1864, and the doors have marbleized ceramic doorknobs (Fig. 7.6C).

During the long period that Herschel and Janie lived in the house, they used the upstairs for storage. This upstairs area is original and clearly displays the fine craftsmanship of the builder. The rooms show 9" to 10" beaded planed planking. The doors are batten design (Fig. 7.6B). The beautiful examples of door mounting hardware are hand-forged straps with eyelet hinges. This same type of hinge is present on the outside shutters (Fig. 7.8D). Each of the upstairs rooms has six windows, and the central hallway has a window at either end. The green and teal blue paint on the stairway and ceiling of the upper floor dates from the twentieth century. The baseboards have a single groove at the top and the ceiling has narrow crown molding. The unadorned fireplace mantels are painted white.[8]

Shortly after Tom McCall moved into the house in 1966, he made significant inside modifications. The changes included adding paneling to the downstairs rooms and enclosing the back shed porch. Tom moved the kitchen to the main part of the house and remodeled a room on the east side of the back porch into a bathroom. He also added closets upstairs and down.[9]

The hand-hewn 9" by 9" foundation sills of the house rest on both heart pine and brick piers. Most of the piers visible around the perimeter of the house are brick, while many of the ones under the interior of the house are heart pine piers (Fig. 7.11B). The floor joists are round logs with the top side flattened to support the floorboards. The builders used numerous wooden shims to level the floor.

The corbel-capped chimneys appear to be original, and represent the only nonreplacement chimneys found during the county survey. The bricks are handmade of local clay and sand. The bricks in the chimney and foundation piers match. A cantilevered roof surrounds the chimney and provides it protection from the weather. There is a wooden support brace extending from both sides of the main roof to the front porch roof (Fig. 7.5A). This feature is unique among the Plantation Plain houses of the county.

All of the windows are six-over-six double-hung sashes. The shutter hinges are still in place and work perfectly (Fig. 7.8C). As late as the 1960s, the downstairs windows had moveable louvered shutters. The solid wooden shutters (Fig. 7.8A) remaining on the detached kitchen have 3" hinges on one side and both they and the latches are hand wrought. Vintage photos of the house show the same type shutters on the upstairs windows (Fig. 7.1). The front door has two-pane sidelights (Fig. 7.9C).

One of the interesting features of the house is that the builder positioned a door on the north side of the east chimney. This door was reconfigured into a window at some later late, reportedly at the request of Janie Durrence who said that she did not like the idea of an outside door opening into her bedroom. There is also evidence that at one time a second front door opened into the west first-floor room of the main part of the house.[10]

The house originally had a detached kitchen/dining room (Fig. 7.7C and D) with a walkway leading to it. Later, a covered, 40' long by 8' wide breezeway attached the main house to the kitchen/dining room. These rooms are of similar size with a door opening between them. The kitchen had a fireplace on the west side, as well as a potbellied stove added later. A close examination reveals that the kitchen/dining room is probably of the same vintage as the house. The dining room has the same type of planking as the main house, but the kitchen has narrower tongue-and-groove wallboards, indicating a re-covering of the kitchen walls at some time.

Most of the farmstead outbuildings are still in place. These include a sugar house, smokehouse, cotton house, and barns. Several are of log construction (Fig. 7.10B) and contain hand-crafted wooden door hinges (Fig. 7.11A). "Residents" of the Durrence barnyard include several peacocks (Fig. 7.10A). Durrence family members state that peacocks have been present on the house grounds since the original owners lived there.[11]

Of special note is the well sweep (Fig. 7.7A), still in working order, in the yard on the east side of the house. It is probably the last one in Evans County and is a vestige of an earlier era when many yard wells had such a device.

Figure 7.2
Elizabeth Grice Durrence and Thomas A. Durrence.
(Photo courtesy of Emily Groover)

Figure 7.3
Grandchildren of Hon. Thomas A. Durrence, 1958. (Photo from Georgia
Department of Archives and History Vanishing Georgia Collection)

Figure 7.4
Durrence House east elevation shows 40' covered walkway (*center*)
leading to dining room/kitchen. (Photo from Savannah College of
Art and Design 1998 survey)

A

Figure 7.5
(A) The Durrence House has a support beam extending from house roof to front porch roof. *(B)* East elevation of the house shows the last known well sweep of its type in Evans County.

B

A

B

Figure 7.6
(A) Central-hall stairs lead from back to front and have railing around upstairs landing.
(B) Upstairs doors are batten construction. *(C)* Many of the doors have porcelain knobs.

C

HOUSES OF HEART PINE

A

B

C

D

Figure 7.7
(A) Well sweep. *(B)* Detail of detached kitchen roof eave.
(C) North elevation of kitchen.
(D) West elevation of kitchen.

A

B

C

Figure 7.8
(A) Wooden shutters still work
perfectly. *(B)* Hand-wrought shutter
latch. *(C)* Shutter hinge base.

D

HOUSES OF HEART PINE

Figure 7.9
(A) Front (south) elevation photographed in 1993.
(B) Roof and wall detail.
(C) Front door with side-lights.

A

B

Figure 7.10
(A) Log outbuilding and ever-
present peacocks on the grounds.
(B) Detail of saddle-notched logs.

A

Figure 7.11
(A) Hand-carved wooden door hinge
on outbuilding. (B) Heart pine piers
under covered breezeway of the
house.

B

Figure 8.1
The Edwards-Strickland House.

8 EDWARDS-STRICKLAND HOUSE

William Henry Edwards, born in South Carolina in 1797, came to Georgia with his grandparents, John and Ursula O'Neill, in 1799. The O'Neills raised William Henry after William's father, mother, and sister died during a fever epidemic in 1797. The O'Neills settled in upper Bryan County, close to the Canoochee River.[1]

O'Neill acquired his lands in the Canoochee River bottoms to take advantage of the fertility and transportation access provided by the nearby waterway. The O'Neill lands, astride the Canoochee and between Bull and Lotts creeks, encompassed property in Bryan County on the east and Tattnall County on the west side of the river. This location is where the present-day Highway 280 bridge crosses the Canoochee three miles east of the town of Daisy in Evans County.[2]

Edwards-Strickland House Floor Plan

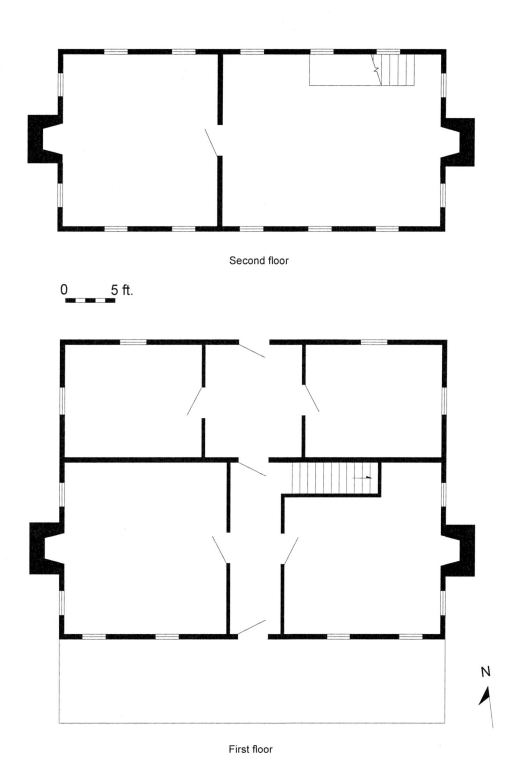

Second floor

0 ____ 5 ft.

First floor

N

Immediately west of these lands was the community of Palatkee, an early Creek Indian settlement. The name Palatkee comes from the Indian word for "crossing or fording place" and is one of the earliest place-names in the area.[3]

Soon after his arrival, O'Neill established a ferry that became an important river crossing for a new road built from the Ohoopee River across Tattnall County and on to Savannah. The Sunbury Road crossed this new Tattnall-Savannah Road nearby (Fig. 8.5) and the location soon became important for both east-west and north-south travel through the backwoods.[4]

By 1820 both of William's grandparents had died, and he inherited their land and enterprises. By that time William was also a veteran of the War of 1812 and the husband of his new bride, Sarah Sands.[5]

In 1821, the Georgia Legislature authorized Edwards to build a toll bridge across the Canoochee at the former site of O'Neill's Ferry (Fig. 8.3). Along with this business, he began to accumulate large land holdings. In addition to 2,778 acres in state land grants, he purchased over 7,000 acres. His vast properties facilitated various other ventures including farming, timbering, and sawmilling.[6]

Edwards's growing family and prosperity prompted the need for a substantial home. By 1846 he owned a two-story house on the Tattnall side of the river. Establishment of this date is via records of a fifa judgment against him by the Central Bank of Georgia and published in the March 10, 1846 edition of the Milledgeville *Southern Recorder* newspaper (Fig. 8.4). The newspaper article lists this two-story house as part of Edwards's property attached by the sheriff. Unless he replaced the house present in 1846 with a new one, the newspaper documentation indicates that Edwards's house is the oldest home in Evans County. The records are not clear on the disposition of the judgement, but it appears there was never an actual sale of the house.[7]

Edwards's sons lived near their father. William Henry Edwards, Jr., known as Henry to distinguish him from William, Sr., operated a store and inn. This rest spot was highly regarded as "a good place to spend the night" in the 1860s by travelers as referenced in the book *The Children of Pride*.[8]

William Edwards was a medical doctor. He practiced, travelling by sulky and on horseback, over a large area including parts of Tattnall, Bryan,

Bulloch, and Liberty counties. In 1872 he suffered a fatal accident when a burning tree fell on his buggy as he was on his way to care for an ailing patient.[9]

After William, Sr.'s death, his youngest son, Thomas J. Edwards, Sr. inherited the house (Fig. 8.7). He and his family lived there until construction of the Savannah and Western Railroad through the area in 1890. At that time they built a house in the new railroad depot town of Daisy located two miles west of their old home. It was Edwards's daughter, Miss Daisy Edwards, for whom residents named the new town. One of Thomas's sons, Charles G. Edwards, served six terms as a U. S. Congressman. Thomas Edwards died in 1921 and a subsequent division of his over 3,000-acre estate left the house in the possession of his descendants for the next 25 years (Fig. 8.8).[10]

The Edwards house remained relatively unmodified until the family sold it in 1946 to J.C. and Julia Strickland. Prior to the sale, the house was vacant for a number of years. During this period it was used as a goat barn and the structure greatly deteriorated. The Stricklands made extensive modifications to make the house livable.[11]

House Survey

The Edwards house is a Plantation Plain form. It has several elements that point to a pre-1850 vintage. The original roof overhang was very narrow, accentuating the house's more vertical profile common to the earlier Federal period (Fig. 8.6). Other details pointing to the earlier era include dentil molding on the cornice and vertical rectangular glass panes on the front door transom (Fig. 8.10).

Edwards had extensive holdings of pine lands and was very active in the timber industry. He operated a sawmill in the Palatkee area in antebellum times and thereafter. It is likely that Edwards sawed the lumber for his house at this sawmill.[12]

The house originally faced south on the Savannah Highway, instead of its current northerly direction. The state rerouted Highway 280 to the north side of the house and paved the road in the early 1930s. In order to reorient the front of the house to the highway, owner J.C. Strickland remodeled the back shed rooms into a front porch and enclosed the old front porch making it the back of the house (Fig. 8.9).[13]

The house is of braced-frame, mortise-and-tenon construction (Fig. 8.12). Horizontal tongue-and-groove planks cover the interior walls of the house and the area under the porch. The house had shutters at one time and most of the handmade hinges are still in place. Shutter ties remain on the upper floor's eastern elevation.

Prior to the renovation, the house was of a central-hall configuration. The stairway led from a doorway in the central hall into the northeast room and up toward the east end of the house. J. C. moved the stairway to the west side of the center hall and eliminated the eastern partition of the hall.[14]

The exterior-end chimneys with fireplaces on both stories were in poor condition, and J. C. razed them. He also demolished the detached kitchen/dining room on the north side of the house. The detached kitchen had an uncovered, ground-level walkway to the main house. J. C. lowered the house from brick piers onto cement blocks. During the renovation, he reused most of the existing material in the house such as windows and doors (Fig. 8.11).[15]

Dreyfus Strickland bought the house in 1957 and made further modifications during the next two years. He extended the roof eaves to provide a larger overhang to deflect water away from the sides of the house. Other changes included replacement of the tin roof with asphalt shingles, installation of paneling, and remodeling the downstairs bathroom. A local contractor, Aubrey Glisson, did the renovation work.[16]

Although twentieth-century changes to the house significantly modified its original plan, the structure's exterior still retains important elements of its Federal-period form. This structure is the county's only surviving dwelling from that earlier era.

Figure 8.2
William H. Edwards, Sr., and Sarah
Sands Edwards. (Photos from *Gene-
alogy of the Edwards Family* by
George Durrence)

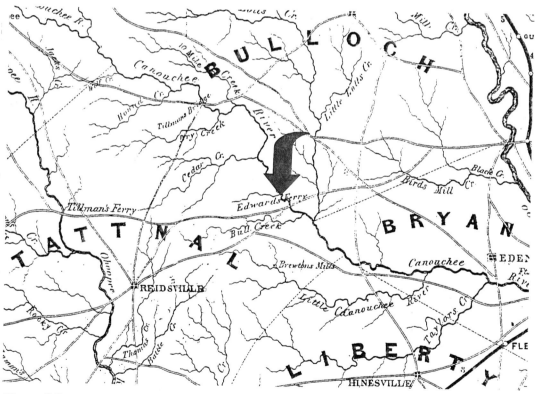

Figure 8.3
Bonner's Pocket Map of the State of Georgia, 1855, shows Edwards Ferry at the important
Savannah Road crossing of the Canoochee River.

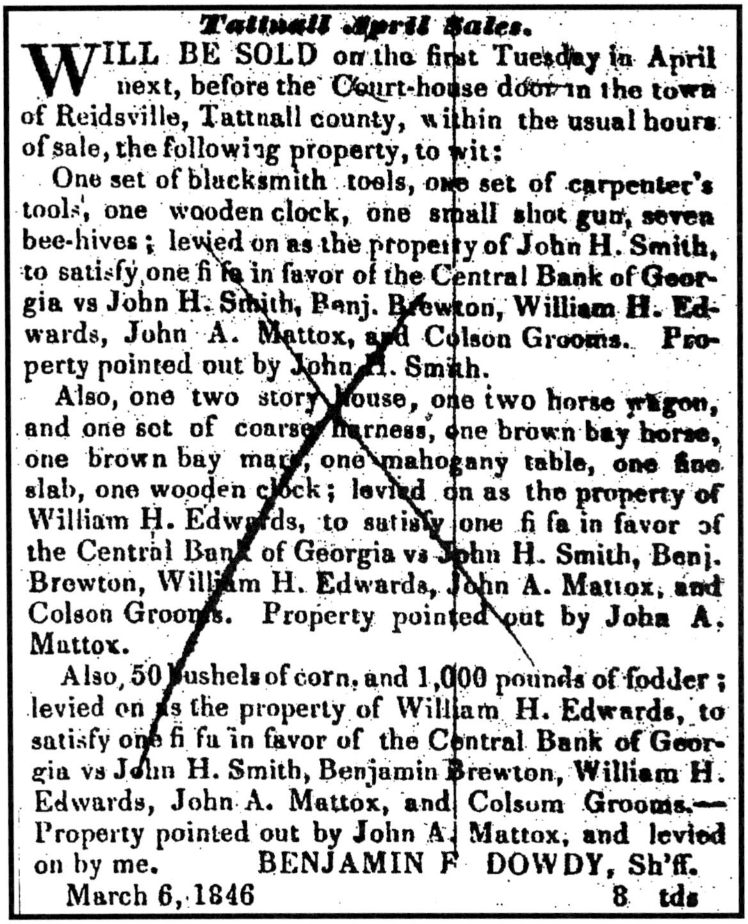

Tattnall April Sales.

WILL BE SOLD on the first Tuesday in April next, before the Court-house door in the town of Reidsville, Tattnall county, within the usual hours of sale, the following property, to wit:

One set of blacksmith tools, one set of carpenter's tools, one wooden clock, one small shot gun, seven bee-hives; levied on as the property of John H. Smith, to satisfy one fi fa in favor of the Central Bank of Georgia vs John H. Smith, Benj. Brewton, William H. Edwards, John A. Mattox, and Colson Grooms. Property pointed out by John H. Smith.

Also, one two story house, one two horse wagon, and one set of coarse harness, one brown bay horse, one brown bay mare, one mahogany table, one fine slab, one wooden clock; levied on as the property of William H. Edwards, to satisfy one fi fa in favor of the Central Bank of Georgia vs John H. Smith, Benj. Brewton, William H. Edwards, John A. Mattox, and Colson Grooms. Property pointed out by John A. Mattox.

Also, 50 bushels of corn, and 1,000 pounds of fodder; levied on as the property of William H. Edwards, to satisfy one fi fa in favor of the Central Bank of Georgia vs John H. Smith, Benjamin Brewton, William H. Edwards, John A. Mattox, and Colsum Grooms.— Property pointed out by John A. Mattox, and levied on by me. BENJAMIN F. DOWDY, Sh'ff.

March 6, 1846   8 tds

Figure 8.4
This newspaper notice, dated March 6, 1846, provides evidence that William H. Edwards, Sr., constructed the house prior to that date.

Figure 8.5
The Edwards House was located near the Sunbury Road.

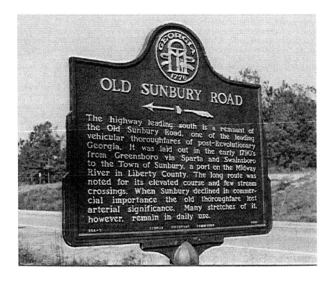

Figure 8.6
A 1952 photograph of the Edwards-Strickland House shows the structure before owners extended the eaves and replaced the roof. Note the more pronounced vertical form indicating Federal-period influence and confirming the house's older vintage. (Photo courtesy of J. C. Strickland)

Figure 8.7
W. F. (*left*) and T. J. Edwards. T. J. inherited the family home place and lived there until the early 1890s. (Photo from *A History of Our Locale*)

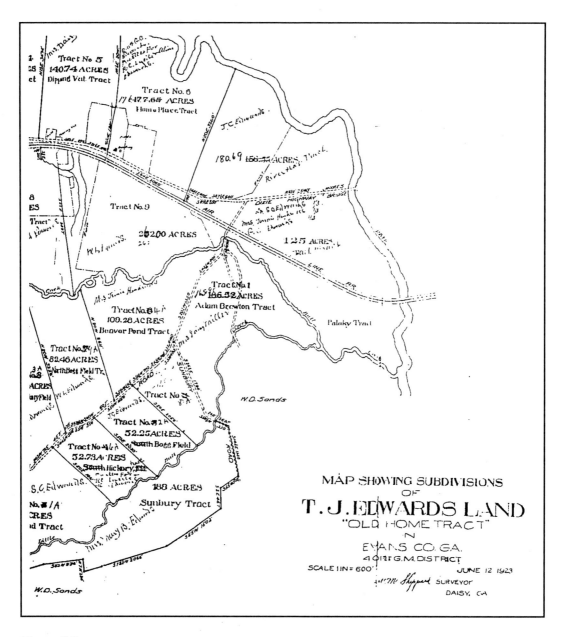

Figure 8.8

By 1840 William H. Edwards acquired, through grant and purchase, 14,517 acres of land in Tattnall, Bulloch, and Bryan counties. He also owned several thousand additional acres in the land lottery counties of Georgia. His youngest son, Thomas J. Edwards, purchased a large tract from his father in 1865. Pictured is a partial plat of Thomas's extensive land holdings that included the site of the Edwards-Strickland House. (Evans County Deed Book 6: 351)

Figure 8.9
Northeast view of house. The current front elevation was formerly the back of the house. A 1930s highway project rerouted the road to the north side of the dwelling, and the owners reoriented the house.

Figure 8.10
House details include dentil molding (*left*) and transom light over the former front doorway.

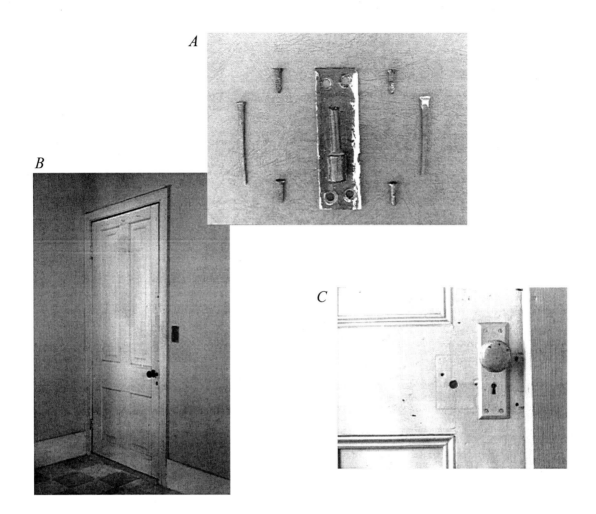

Figure 8.11
(A) Window shutter mount, screws, and cut nails used in the house.
(B) Hand-crafted door. *(C)* Detail of door and later-vintage replacement knob.

A

B

Figure 8.12
(A) Hand-numbered rafters are visible from the front porch.
(B) The house is of upbraced, frame construction.

Figure 9.1
The John Rogers House.

9 JOHN "DUFFY" ROGERS HOUSE

The son of Uriah and Martha Brewton Rogers, John "Duffy" Rogers (1847-1941) grew up in Bulloch County on his family's farm just over the then Bulloch/Tattnall county line near the mouth of Lotts Creek on the Canoochee River.

John Rogers joined the Georgia Militia in June 1864 at the age of 16. At his death in 1941, Rogers was Evans County's oldest living Confederate veteran. He also had the distinction of living in what is now one of the county's oldest houses.[1]

In 1870, Duffy bought 380 acres containing the house site in Tattnall (now Evans) County from his brother, James J. Rogers. The state of Georgia originally granted this tract to John DeLoach in 1835. Subsequent to DeLoach, owners were Duffy's uncle, Samuel Brewton, and later, Duffy's father, Uriah.

John Rogers House Floor Plan

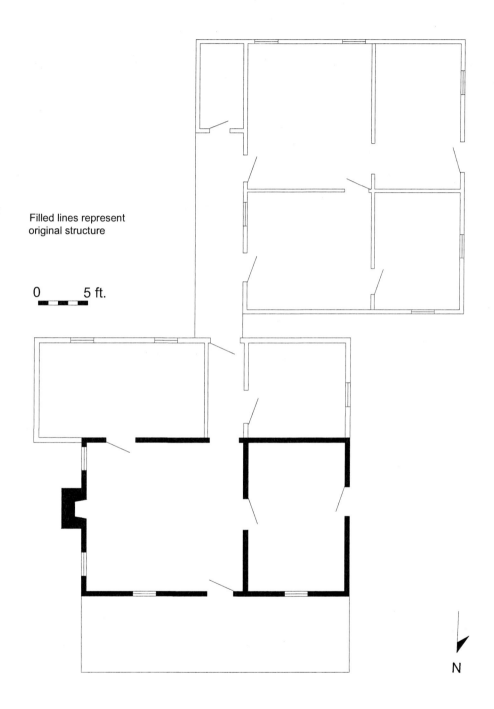

Filled lines represent
original structure

0   5 ft.

N

The Uriah to James property sale took place in 1866, and family tradition holds that the log house was on the site at the time of the purchase. Because of the dearth of construction during the war years of 1861 to 1865, the original part of the house is almost certainly antebellum.[2]

Over the course of his life, John Rogers had three wives and 20 children. His spouses were Laura Blitch (1852-1883), Melvina Hearn (1861-1927), and Elizabeth Spear.[3]

Duffy was very active in religious affairs, and was instrumental in the establishment of Bull Creek Church. He donated the land and assisted in the construction of the building. Despite his stewardship at the church, however, a dispute arose over the support of foreign missions, and Duffy moved his membership to Bay Branch Church in protest.[4]

In 1932, John Rogers gave the house and 90 acres to his daughter, Susan Hester. Susan sold the home to her nephew Ulysess Rogers in 1957. His widow, Sybble, owned the dwelling for a number of years, and their son John Rogers of Walthourville now owns it.[5]

Family members relate that the first 13 children were born in the house, and John enlarged it to accommodate his growing family. The family moved into a much larger house two miles east of the log home in approximately 1891.[6]

Duffy is perhaps one of the most colorful individuals ever to live in Evans County. His exploits as a Confederate soldier, his exciting days rafting logs on the river, his notable disagreements over proper church doctrine, and his many family connections make him well known in the history of the area.

House Survey

An original log structure is the nucleus of the house. The log section is a double pen, with one room measuring 17' by 16' attached to a second room measuring 13' by 16'. Saddle joints connect the logs. At some date after original construction, a vertical board was placed over the ends of the logs and spike nails hammered into them (Fig. 9.5B) to help prevent shifting. The spaces between the logs have narrow boards nailed into them for chinking.

Other elements of the house include a front porch roof that has a continuous, hand-hewn beam 36' 6" long. The roof, originally covered with wood shakes, now has asphalt shingles. The house's interior walls are covered with a ¼" painted panel board.

It appears that the west side of the log wall included a door at one time (Fig. 9.7). Duffy later filled in the door with a window, perhaps at the time that he added the rear rooms. A small shed porch roof remains on the west elevation as a further indication that the opening was once used as an entry point.

Duffy expanded the original log house with a rear addition and a kitchen (Fig. 9.4). A small porch joins the two sections of the house. The foundation beneath the original log structure and the kitchen building are of the same vintage. This configuration indicates that Duffy raised the original log structure at the time the additions were made. The sills are hand-hewn and sit on tall brick piers (Fig. 9.3C). The floor joists are round logs with hewn ends and flattened top edges (Fig. 9.3A). The floorboards rest on the joists' flat surface and those on the porch, back section of the log house, and the kitchen building match. The boards comprising the floor of the east room of the log house, however, are different, indicating older vintage.

This type of log house plan must have been popular in the area, as the Amos Hearn log structure in the Bellville area had an almost exact configuration (see Chapter 12). Additionally, it is interesting to note that the older part of the nearby Bull Creek Baptist Church has an identical foundation system as that found in the Rogers house. Rogers's connection with the construction of both structures is likely.

The original chimney was "stick-and-clay" as evidenced by the clay still affixed to the logs behind the chimney stack (Fig. 9.7B). The composition of the brick and mortar used in the chimney and foundation piers mark them as a later addition. Remnants of the previously used handmade bricks are still under the house (Fig. 9.6B).

A dominant feature of the house is the cantilevered roof (Fig. 9.6A) common on many log houses of nineteenth-century Georgia. This 6' wide overhang provided the clay chimney protection from the rain. When these chimneys caught fire, it was usually from the inner hearth firebox itself rather than the part protruding through the roof. Therefore, the cantilevered roof chimney arrangement was not as great a fire hazard as it would appear.

The front porch has six chamfered support posts and the porch rafters remain exposed. The front elevation contains a center door with windows on either side.

The Duffy Rogers home is one of the few early log structures left in Evans County. The house form with its dominating roof line and elevated piers seems perfectly sited on a slight hill at a pronounced curve on Rogers Road. The charm of the house is a tribute to one of Evans County's most respected and influential citizens.

A

B

Figure 9.2
(A) John "Duffy" Rogers. (Photo
courtesy of Georgia Department of
Archives and History Vanishing Georgia
Collection.) *(B)* Rogers's second wife,
Melvina Hearn Rogers. (Photo from *A
History of Our Locale.)*

A

Figure 9.3
(A) Log joists with flattened
tops support floorboards.
(B) Spike nails fasten a
support board to the end of
the logs. *(C)* Lapped joint
connects porch sills. Brick
piers are 36" tall.

B

C

Figure 9.4
Two views of detached
kitchen on south side of
main house.

Figure 9.5
West wall of
house has
window in
original door
opening.

A

Figure 9.6
(A) East elevation showing cantilevered roof. *(B)* Clay
from former clay-and-stick chimney is visible behind the
chimney stack. *(C)* Handmade "sand" brick.

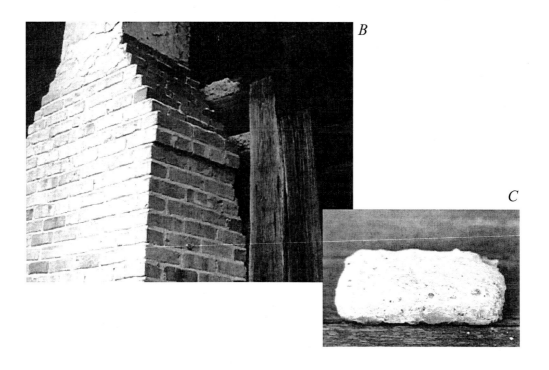

B

C

Figure 9.7
View of northwest corner of the house.

Figure 10.1
The Thomas E. Rogers House.

10   THOMAS E. ROGERS HOUSE

Thomas E. Rogers (1832-1864) was the oldest child of Uriah A. Rogers (1809-1882) and Martha Brewton Rogers (1813-1890). Martha was the daughter of Nathan and Nancy Brewton. Uriah Rogers was the son of Thomas Rogers and Asha Everitt Rogers. Thomas E. Rogers grew up in Bulloch County (now Evans) on the west side of Lotts Creek near the point where this tributary enters the Canoochee River.[1]

Thomas Rogers's father owned more than 10,000 acres in Bulloch and Tattnall counties, and Thomas's grandfather, Nathan Brewton, owned a similar amount. Thomas moved to adjoining Tattnall County and became a farmer. He married Caroline Bacon (1838-1854) in 1853. His second marriage was to Charity Kicklighter (1833-1896) in 1854. Thomas and Charity were the parents of six children.[2]

Uriah Rogers gave his son Thomas 370 acres on Little Bull Creek in then Tattnall County in 1857. Family tradition holds that Thomas built the house fairly soon after the land was given to him. Based on Thomas's tax

Thomas E. Rogers House Floor Plan

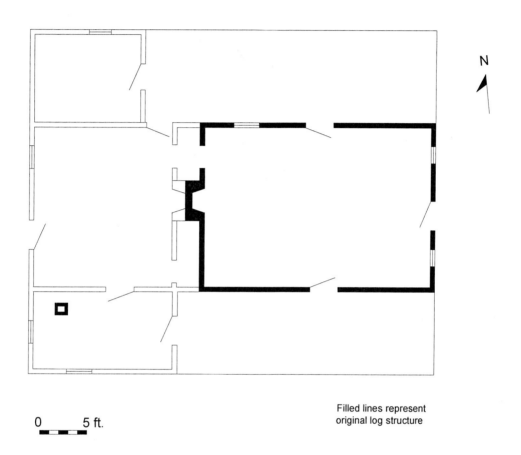

Filled lines represent
original log structure

0 ___ 5 ft.

returns in the Tattnall County digest, the year of construction was probably late 1858 or 1859.[3]

A chain-of-title search on the land where the house is sited reveals that the state originally granted this land to John Harrell in 1806. At the time of the grant, the parcel was part of Liberty County (now Evans County). By 1853, a land speculator, Ebenezer Jencks, owned the property. Among other ventures, Jencks was the promoter of the Savannah-Ogeechee-Altamaha Canal enterprise. In 1856, he sold 6,459 acres, which included this 370 acres, to Samuel Brewton. Samuel Brewton sold this land to his brother-in-law, Uriah Rogers in 1856. A year later, Uriah gave the land to his son Thomas Rogers.[4]

Following Thomas's death during the War Between the States, Charity next married John W. Martin. John was a fellow soldier in Thomas's regiment during the war. John died in 1893, and Charity apparently continued to live in the house until her death in 1896. Their youngest child, William, bought the land and house from his mother and siblings and resided there until his death in 1915. William's youngest child, Charity, who married Arlie Todd, bought the house and land in 1920. Family tradition states that Charity drew straws with her siblings and won the right to obtain the home place tract. Charity's son, Donnie Todd, acquired the property in 1971. His daughter Janean Coe bought the house in 1996 and is the current owner. The house and land, therefore, remains in the family of the original builder.[5]

Thomas Rogers (3rd Sgt.) was a member of Company B of the 7th Georgia Cavalry. He was captured June 11, 1864 at Louisa Court House, Virginia, during the Battle of Trevillian Station. He was one of about 180 members of the 7th captured at that battle and sent via Point Lookout Prison in Maryland to Elmira Prison in New York. Thomas's brother and fellow member of the regiment, Alexander C. Rogers, was also captured during the same battle. The conditions at Elmira Prison were notoriously harsh and Thomas's health apparently deteriorated during his stay. Perhaps because of his poor physical condition, he was subject to a prisoner exchange October 11, 1864. He died, however, in a Federal hospital two days later in Baltimore, Maryland. He is buried in Lauden Park Cemetery in Baltimore.[6]

Many owners of nineteenth-century log houses expanded the structures as their families grew and resources increased. Rather than a rear addition such as that built in the nearby John Rogers House (see Chapter 9), the Thomas Rogers house addition is located on the side of the original log structure.

The original log section of the house is a 16' by 24' single-pen. The older part of the house contains mortise-and-tenon joinery and the newer part has framed lumber and nails (Fig. 10.5*D*). The windows in this older portion do not have panes and are covered by wooden shutters (Fig. 10.3*B*). Saddle notching connects the 8" diameter unhewn logs (Fig. 10.4*B*), and thin wooden slats wedged between the logs comprise the chinking. Family lore reveals this chinking was used for purposes other than filling the space between the logs. William Rogers reportedly acquired the nickname "Stingy Bill" from his habit of keeping his money stashed between these log walls.[7]

The owner expanded the log structure by adding two rooms on the west side of the house. To accommodate this addition, the single fireplace was replaced with a double fireplace (Fig. 10.6). One of the fireplaces faced the one-room log portion of the house and the other serviced the new frame-constructed room. A back room used as a kitchen was also added to the structure. Bricks for a cook-stove chimney are still present in the kitchen roof. The front of the addition forms a "parson's room" with a door leading to the porch.

The hand-hewn sills sit on tapered heart pine blocks (Fig. 10.3*C*). The replacement gable roof is corrugated tin, and 4" diameter poles comprise the rafters. Laths nailed to the poles provide additional stability. Five-inch planks comprise the floors and ceiling. There is evidence of rudimentary electrical wiring.

The front porch shed roof is offset below the gable roof over the main section of the house. A later-added shed roof also spanned the back porch the length of the log structure. This roof extended from the edge of the kitchen to the east end of the log house.

Occupied until the early 1950s, the dwelling was last used as a tenant house. The west end of the house is badly deteriorated and leaning severely in that direction. Although the house is in ruins, the remnants give a clear picture of the once-common log houses of the area. As seen in several other examples in this section of the state, farmers extended the life of their log houses by enlarging them with frame add-ons.[8]

A

B

C

Figure 10.2
(A) Thomas E. Rogers.
(B) Thomas's first wife,
Caroline Bacon. *(C)* Charity
Kicklighter, second wife of
Thomas Rogers. (Photos on
this page courtesy of
Dorothy Simmons)

Figure 10.3
Hartridge and Macy Ann Rogers Durrence, the daughter
of Thomas and Charity Rogers. Family tradition holds
she was the first of the children born in the log house.
(Photo courtesy of Dorothy Simmons)

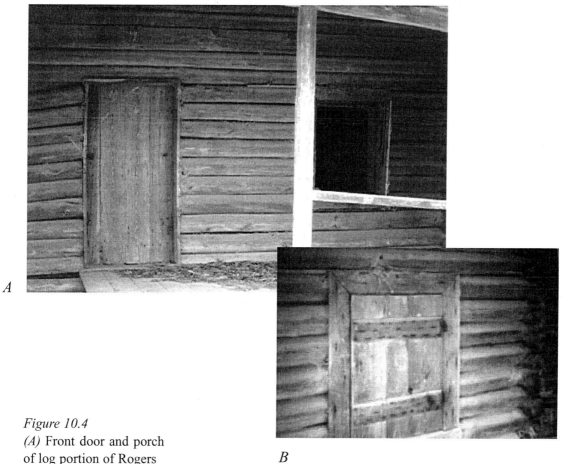

A

B

Figure 10.4
(A) Front door and porch
of log portion of Rogers
house. *(B)* Detail of front
shutter. *(C)* Tapered heart
pine blocks serve as piers
for foundation of both the
log house and addition.

C

A

B

C

Figure 10.5
(A) South (back) elevation
of log house. *(B)* Southeast corner of log house
showing window place-
ment. *(C)* and *(D)* Door
frame detail of south
(back) elevation.

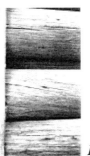

D

HOUSES OF HEART PINE

A

B

Figure 10.6
(A) Detail of fireplace and adjoining wall. *(B)* Interior view of fireplace. *(C)* Part of the doorway of log portion of house. *(D)* North elevation detail showing connecting point of older log house and newer frame addition.

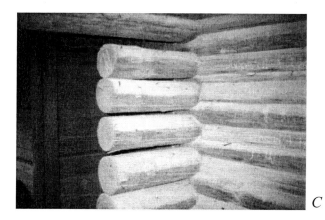

C

D

Figure 11.1
The Smith-Daniel House in 1997.

11   SMITH-DANIEL HOUSE

James B. Smith (1823-1891) was the son of James and Frances Bell Smith, and the grandson of Simon and Mary Smith. Simon Smith was a Revolutionary War soldier from North Carolina who received a bounty land grant in Washington County, Georgia, for his service. After acquiring additional grants in Burke and Screven counties, he settled in Tattnall County in the early 1820s. He was the patriarch of one of the two large nineteenth-century Smith families residing in the portion of the county that became Evans in 1914. The Smith family owned thousands of acres of land extending from present-day Bellville in Evans County south to Bull Creek.[1]

SMITH-DANIEL HOUSE FLOOR PLAN

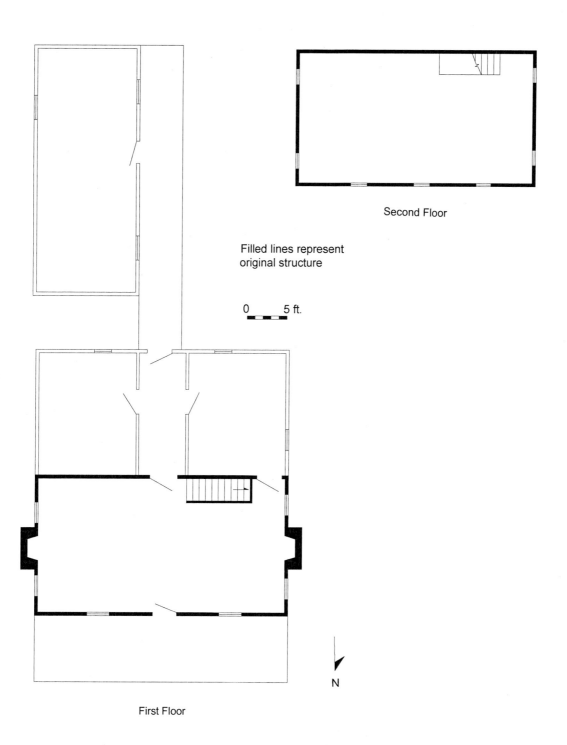

Second Floor

Filled lines represent
original structure

0   5 ft.

N

First Floor

James Smith lived in Screven County and immigrated to Tattnall about 1803. He was a planter and married Frances Bell in 1800. Their son, James B. Smith, was the youngest of eight children.[2]

James B. Smith married Georgia Ann Sikes (1825-1870) in 1840. After her death, he married Rachel Tippins (1834-1900) in 1872. By 1843, he had accumulated over 3,000 acres of land. He represented Tattnall County in the Georgia Legislature from 1855 to 1858 and again in 1877. Smith also served as Tattnall Clerk of Superior Court in 1854. He entered the War Between the States as a captain in the 61st Georgia Regiment. After the war, he was one of the founding trustees of the Tattnall County Campground.[3]

In 1851, James B. Smith bought 25 acres on the "road leading from Reidsville to Savannah" from Benjamin Brewton. The state originally granted this land to Charles Mulford in 1814. It was upon these lands that Smith constructed his house circa 1856.[4]

James B. Smith owned this land until his death in 1891. His son, Pulaski Sikes Smith, (known as "Sikes"), was next to own the house and land. Sikes died in 1894 and his widow, Mary Eliza Tippins Smith, continued to live in the house. The house and land remained as Pulaski Sikes Smith estate property until Helen Daniel, a daughter of Sikes, acquired the undivided interests of her siblings. In 1954, Helen sold the house and surrounding 61 acres of land to her son, Walter Emmett Daniel, whose family retains it to the present.[5]

House Survey

The house shows a sturdy story-and-a-half floor plan. It began as a single-pen log house that was expanded with rear shed rooms giving it the external look of a Plantation Plain structure. This structurally sound log house has many features that make it unique to the county. First, most log structures of the area were single story versus the extra half-story present in this structure. Secondly, the full-dovetail notches (Fig. 11.4B) that connect the squared logs (Fig. 11.5B) were common above Georgia's fall line, but much rarer in South Georgia. The dovetails provide increased strength and durability for the joints. These notches are reinforced with wooden pegs and, in some locations, further secured with iron spike nails. The back shed rooms of this structure are much larger in proportion to the main front rooms than in the Plantation Plain houses of the county. These rear rooms are also of a later vintage than the front log section of the structure. The farmstead has numerous outbuildings including barns, cribs, sheds, and a tobacco barn.[6]

The foundation sills sit on brick piers. There appear to be at least two previous foundation systems. During a 1997 renovation, workers found cypress blocks that were probably the original piers for the house. At some later date, these blocks were replaced with brick piers. The first brick piers were four feet or more in height. A long-time owner of the house, Walter Emmett Daniel, remembered when the elevated height of the house allowed storage of buggies and bales of cotton underneath. Workers lowered the house to its present level concurrently with rebuilding the chimneys.[7]

The tapered columns on the full-width front porch appear to be original and provide the structure's only external ornamentation (Fig. 11.7A). The porch rails are set into vertical boards on either side of the columns. Connected with mortise and tenon, these boards allow attachment of the rails without weakening the columns (Fig. 11.7B).

Some of the batten doors are original to the house and have handmade, hook-and-eye latches and porcelain door knobs (Fig. 11.7C). The doors also had wooden latches at one time (Fig. 11.7D). The woodwork is unpainted and highlights the heart pine's rich brown-red patina.

Access to the upper floor is by uncased stairs (Fig. 11.6D). The stairs are now enclosed at the top, but originally had a mortise-and-tenon secured handrail from the bottom to the top of the stairs and around the stair opening in the upper floor. The upstairs is one large room measuring 30' by 16' and is covered by 9" plank flooring. The height from the floor to the top of the ridgeplate is 6' 2". The upstairs west end wall bears a series of vertical auger holes indicating unexecuted plans for a fireplace.

The upstairs exposed rafters and roofing form the ceiling. There are three 2' by 3' unglazed window openings with batten wooden shutters (Fig. 11.5A). The 6" by 6" ridgeplate is 36' in length (Fig. 11.6C). The gable ends of the house have two vertical supports, or queen posts, (Fig. 11.6A) and there are collar beams on three of the rafter pairs. A cantilevered roof surrounds and protects the chimney (Fig. 11.4*C*). The original rafters were hand-hewn and had a lath system on which to place the wood shingles. There have been three generations of roof covering: wood shingles, crimped tin, and the current asphalt shingles.[8]

The framed construction detached kitchen is of a later period than the main house (Fig.11.8). The interior has beaded, tongue-and-groove boards indicating a late nineteenth-century addition. There is evidence of a flue stack for a wood burning stove. The Smiths later used this structure as a dormitory for the children, and it was known as the "boys' house." At the time of the renovation in 1998, there was no evidence the kitchen/dormitory had ever had electricity.[9]

The 1998 restoration of the main house included removing interior paneling to expose logs, jacking parts of the structure to stabilize it, and replacing some of the sills and joists. Additionally, workers placed a new roof on the house.

The Walter Emmett Daniel family, owners of the home since 1954, uses the dwelling as a guest house. This unpretentious home with its unpainted exterior and sturdy construction stands as a tribute to a simpler time when log structures dominated the rural landscape of the area that is now Evans County.

Figure 11.2
James B. Smith. (Photo courtesy
of Walter Emmett Daniel)

Figure 11.3
The Daniel-Smith-
Tippins Cemetery
located just north
of the Smith-Daniel
House is the burial
place of James B.
Smith and many of
his descendants.

A

Figure 11.4
(A) The main part of the house is log construction while the
back lean-to is framed lumber. *(B)* Full-dovetail joints
connect logs. *(C)* Cantilevered roof surrounds the chimney
stack. *(D)* Fireplace during 1998 renovation.

B

C

D

A

Figure 11.5
(A) Wooden shutters cover
unglazed upstairs windows.
(B) Adz marks are visible on hand-
hewn logs of interior wall.

B

Figure 11.6
(A) Ceiling of upstairs room is formed by open rafters.
(B) Side wall of room is one-half story. *(C)* Top log of
wall serves as ridgeplate. *(D)* Uncased stairs lead to room.

_A_

_B_

Figure 11.7
_(A)_ Wooden peg secures front porch column to ridge plate. _(B)_ Mortis-and-tenon porch rail support. _(C)_ Hand-wrought latch and porcelain doorknob. _(D)_ Wooden door latch.

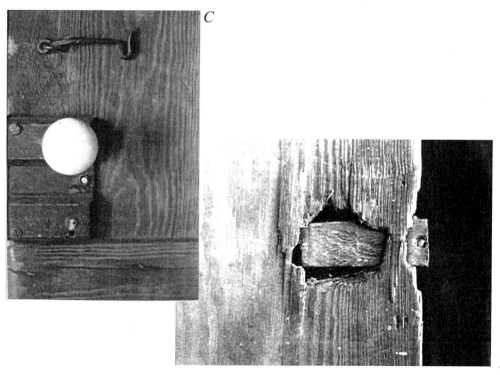

_C_

_D_

Figure 11.8
Two views of the kitchen. Room is connected to the main house by an elevated walkway.

Figure 12.1
Nancy Eulalia Hearn and Amos J. Hearn c.1860.
(Photo courtesy of Emily Groover)

12   AMOS J. HEARN

Amos J. Hearn (1824-1864) was one of the most accomplished carpenters in Tattnall County during the 1850s. As builder of the A. D. Eason house in Undine and the J. B. Brewton House, Hearn demonstrated considerable skills. Local historians consider the Eason house to be the finest of its type in the county.

Born the son of Jesse and Lucita Hearn in Twiggs County, Georgia, Amos remained there until the early 1850s. He was already a full-fledged carpenter by the age of 24, and the 1850 census lists him accordingly. Although the records are not definitive, it appears Amos may have learned his trade from his father. Among the items in Jesse Hearn's estate in 1849 that pointed to carpentry skills were augers, drawing knives, axes, iron wedges, chop axe hammers, crowbars, handsaws, squares, planes, and foot adzes.[1]

Amos Hearn married Nancy E. Brewton (1843-1927) in 1859 and completed his own home by 1860. In that year he paid taxes on 400 acres located on what is now the south side of Highway 280 at the Evans/Tattnall county line. He acquired this land from his father-in-law, Simon J. Brewton. Despite his considerable skills as a carpenter, Amos's dwelling was a simple log house (Fig. 12.2).[2]

Hearn started building the A. D. Eason house in July 1856 and completed it in the same month of the following year. Although undocumented, local sources credit Hearn with building the Jonathan Brewton house. This is plausible timewise because the Brewton house was likely constructed in the late 1850s.

According to the 1860 Tattnall County Tax Digest, Amos had one slave. The slave's value in the digest was $1,800. This amount greatly exceeds the average of approximately $1,200 for male slaves. This would probably mean the slave worked alongside Amos and was a skilled carpenter in his own right.[3]

Hearn was apparently proud of his work on the Eason house. He boldly signed his name in chalk in the rafters (Fig. 12.3). Local lore indicates that to celebrate the completion of the house's construction, he climbed to the top of the roof and stood on his head.[4]

Amos J. Hearn's carpentry vocation was cut short by the War Between the States. He left his Tattnall County home in Oct 1862 and enlisted in Company H, 5th Georgia Cavalry at South Newport, in McIntosh County. After various postings in Georgia and South Carolina, the Confederate commanders ordered the 5th Georgia to Jacksonville, Florida, in February 1864. As the unit passed through Savannah, it left behind the sick. Among them was Hearn. Amos died in Savannah's Mercy Hospital in April of 1864.[5]

Amos Hearn had the distinction of having had three burials. He was first interred in Savannah during the war. His wife went to Savannah and brought his body back to the homestead and buried him there. In 1959, to insure continued care for his place of burial, his descendants removed his body to Brewton Cemetery in Hagan.[6]

Hearn's untimely death ended an accomplished career that had further promise. His masterpiece, the A. D. Eason House, is the finest antebellum structure in the county and one that shows attention to detail and craftsmanship of the highest order.

Figure 12.2
The Amos J. Hearn House was a log
structure with frame addition. (Photo
from *A History of Our Locale*)

Figure 12.3
Amos Hearn signed
his name boldly in
A. D. Eason's
account book.
(Copy courtesy of
Margaret Eason)

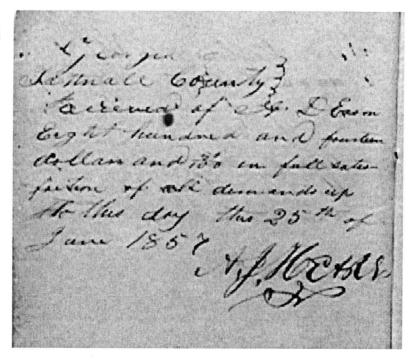

NOTES

Introduction

1. For the purposes of this study, the antebellum period is defined as 1820-1860.

2. John P. Rabun, Jr., *A History of Tattnall County, 1801-1865*, (Privately published, 1954), 25.

3. *Soil Survey of Candler, Evans, and Tattnall Counties* (Washington D.C.: U.S. Department of Agriculture, 1980), 2.

4. Travis C. McDonald, Jr., "Understanding Old buildings: The Process of Architectural Investigation," *Preservation Brief 35*, (Washington: National Park Service Preservation, 2000), 8.

Chapter 1 *Plantation Plain Architecture in Georgia*

1. Six of the structures generally identified as Plantation Plain include two that do not meet the strict definition of the type. The Smith-Daniel House is one room over one room and the Berry Brewton House has one room on the second floor. These houses retain the overall external form of the Plantation Plain.

2. "Georgia's Living Places: Historic Houses in Their Landscaped Setting," Georgia Department of Natural Resources Historic Preservation Section (Atlanta: Georgia Department of Natural Resources, n.d.), I-21.

3. John V. Allcott, *Colonial Homes in North Carolina* (Raleigh: Carolina Center for Tercentenary Commission, 1963), 61; Robert Gamble, *The Alabama Catalog* (Tuscaloosa: University of Alabama Press, 1987), 29; *Historic Preservation Handbook*, Historic Preservation Section (Atlanta: Georgia Depart-

ment of Natural Resources, 1976), 41; Virginia and Lee McAlester, *A Field Guide to American Houses* (New York: Alfred A. Knoph, 1995), 80.

4. *Historic Preservation Handbook*, Historic Preservation Section (Atlanta: Georgia Department of Natural Resources, 1976), 41.

5. Ibid.

6. Frederick Doveton Nichols, *Early Architecture of Georgia* (Savannah: Beehive Press, 1976), 129.

7. Harold Bush-Brown, *Outline of the Development of Early American Architecture: The Southern States, District – Georgia* (Washington, D.C: H.A.B.S, 1936), 16. Copy at Georgia Technical Institute Library, Atlanta.

8. Fred B. Kniffen, "Folk Housing: Key to Diffusion," *Annals of the Association of American Geographers*, December 1965, 549-577.

9. Ibid.

10. Ibid.

11. William Cobbett, *An Epitome of Mr. Forsyth's Treatise on the Culture and Management of Fruit Trees* (Philadelphia: Wm. Poyntell and Co., 1804), 185-186.

12. T. T. Waterman and F. B. Johnston, *Early Architecture of North Carolina* (Chapel Hill: University of N.C. Press, 1941), 41-42; Andrea Niles and Davina Rochlin, *Architecture in Georgia; The Evolution of the Porch,* Pamphlet No. 3 (Atlanta: Georgia Trust for Historic Preservation, 1979).

13. Doug Swaim, "North Carolina Folk Housing," ed. Doug Swaim, *Carolina Dwelling* (Raleigh: N.C. State University School of Design Student Publication, 1978), 38; Dell Upton, "Vernacular Architecture," eds. Roller, David and Robert Twyman, *Encyclopedia of Southern Architecture* (Baton Rouge: Louisiana State University Press, 1989), 110-113.

14. Dell Upton, "Vernacular Architecture," eds. Roller, David and Robert Twyman, *Encyclopedia of Southern Architecture* (Baton Rouge: Louisiana State University Press, 1989), 110-113.

15. Henry Forman, *The Architecture of the Old South: The Medieval Style, 1585-1850* (Cambridge, Massachusetts: Harvard University Press, 1948), 183-184; Jacob Ernest Cook, ed., *Encyclopedia of North American Colonies*, Vol. 3 (New York: Scribners, 1993); Harold D. Eberlein and Cortlandt Van Dyke

Hubbard, *American Georgian Architecture* (New York: Da Capo Press, 1976), 53-55.

16. Doug Swaim, "North Carolina Folk Housing," in *Carolina Dwelling* (Raleigh: N.C. State University School of Design Student Publication, 1978), 38.

17. Robert Winebarger, "The Thomas Redman Thornton House as a Survival of English Folk Architecture in Georgia," manuscript obtained from Building Curator, Stone Mountain Park, Ga. "Take a Stroll Through History at the Antebellum Plantation," Brochure, n. d., Stone Mountain State Park.

18. "Eagle Tavern," (Atlanta: The Georgia Historical Commission, n.d.).

19. "Washington-Wilkes Hosts the Bicentennial Tour of Callaways in Wilkes County," Callaway Family Association, Inc., October 14, 1983. Copy obtained from Callaway Plantation, Washington, Ga.

20. Clyde Hollingsworth, "A Worthy House," n. p., n. d., Copy obtained from "Architectural" vertical file, Bulloch County Library.

21. "Traveler's Rest," Georgia Department of Natural Resources, Atlanta, n. d.; Stephens County roadside marker at State Historic Site, "Traveler's Rest-Old Tugaloo Town."

22. Jonathan Hale, *The Old Way of Seeing* (Boston: Houghton Mifflin Company, 1994), 2.

23. Ibid., 58.

Chapter 2 *Housing in Antebellum Tattnall and Bulloch Counties*

1. Map adapted from David Roller and Robert Twyman, eds. *Encyclopedia of Southern Culture* (Baton Rouge: Louisiana State University Press, 1989), 536; Henry Lionel Williams and Ottalie K. Williams, *A Guide to Old American Houses 1700-1900* (New York: A.S. Barnes and Company, Inc., 1962), 22; Charles F. Kovacik, *South Carolina: A Geography* (Boulder: Westview Press, Inc., 1987), 123; Lucile Hodges, *A History of Our Locale – Mainly Evans County Georgia* (Macon: Southern Press, Inc., 1965), 8.

2. Avis Bacon, interview with author, Claxton, Ga., December 17, 2000.

3. Basil Hall, *Travels in North America* (Edinburgh, 1833), 76, as included in *Rambler in Georgia*, Mills Lane, (Savannah: Beehive Press, 1973); Julia Harn, "Houses," Georgia Historical Quarterly, Vol. 25, No. 1, March 1941, 77-79; James C. Bonner, *A History of Georgia Agriculture, 1732-1860* (Athens: University of Georgia Press, 1964), 177.

4. Brooks and Leodel Coleman, *The Story of Bulloch* (Statesboro, Ga.: Bulloch County Historical Society, 1973), 31.

5. Listed age could be plus or minus one year.

6. From 1860 Tax Digest of Tattnall County and 1860 Census of Bulloch County.

7. Improved and unimproved land holdings listed in 1860 Georgia Agricultural census, Tattnall and Bulloch counties.

8. From 1860 Georgia Slave Schedule, Tattnall and Bulloch counties.

9. First paternal ancestor in Georgia.

10. All offices in Tattnall County except W. H. Edwards, in Bryan, and S. J. Brewton, in Bulloch. Extracted from listing in Hodges, *Our Locale*, 178-183.

11. Date based on 1846 lawsuit that refers to Edwards's two-story house. See Edwards-Strickland House, Chapter 8.

12. The age of the house based on 1846 construction date. We know, however, Edwards probably constructed the house prior to that date.

13. Berry Brewton did not buy the land and house until 1860. He was 26 at the time.

14. Twenty-one of these slaves belonged to the Nathan Brewton, Sr. estate and were not formally distributed to the heirs until 1863. Nathan Brewton, Sr. Estate Records, 1863, Bulloch County Probate Office.

15. John Rogers bought the land and log house in 1870 when he was 23.

16. Measurements rounded to nearest foot. Does not include area of front porch.

17. Refers to the main part of house and does not include rooms on front porch. *Left* and *right* descriptions for orientation viewing the house from front facade.

18. Represents window configuration found in current survey.

19. The Berry Brewton House is the smallest Plantation Plain house in the survey. It originally had two small rooms in the downstairs main part of the house, but wall partition removal was the result of twentieth-century alterations. The upstairs configuration has always been one room versus the normal two-room arrangement for this house type.

20. Red spray-painted in twentieth century.

21. This log house has pronounced Plantation Plain exterior elevations, but lacks the typical two-room over two-room configuration. It has one room above and one room below in the main part of the house. In effect, it is a story-and-half single-pen log house modified by adding a full-width front porch and back lean-to shed rooms.

22. 1850 and 1860 Georgia censuses for Tattnall and Bulloch counties.

23. Ibid.

24. Bulloch County Probate Office Estate Records, S. J. Brewton and Nathan Brewton estate papers.

25. George White, *Statistics of the State of Georgia* (Savannah: W. Thorne Williams, 1849), 116, 535; Hodges, *Locale*, 54-55.

26. 1880 Manufacturing Census, Tattnall County; Theodore Brewton, interview with Charles Johnson, January 29, 1963. Typescript in author's files.

27. General references for this section include: Rita Turner Wall, "Genesis of the Southern Plantation House," n.d., typescript copy in Bulloch County Library Architectural vertical file; John Lindley, *Architecture of Middle Georgia* (Athens: University of Georgia Press, 1972); Gabrielle Lanier and Bernard Herman, *Everyday Architecture in the Middle Atlantic States* (Baltimore: Johns Hopkins University Press, 1997); and the Evans County field surveys conducted by author.

28. Ibid.

29. Ibid.

30. "An Old Georgian," *The Calhoun Times,* April 9, 1875.

31. Wall, "Southern Plantation House," 6-7; Lanier and Herman, *Everyday Architecture in the Middle Atlantic States*, 77-94.

32. Wallace Parker, interview with author, Claxton, Ga., October 3, 2000; "Other Towns Once Prospered in Evans Area," *The Claxton Enterprise*, August 3, 1989, 20.

Chapter 3 Abraham D. Eason House

1. Eason also helped establish Shiloh and Harmony churches in Tattnall County. George F. Austin, *One Hundred Years of Methodism in Tattnall County*

Georgia (Reidsville: Journal Print, 1908), 8-10; Annie B. Eason, *History of Eason's Chapel United Methodist Church, 1880-1980* (Reidsville: *The Tattnall Journal*, n.d.), 7.

2. Austin, *Methodism in Tattnall County Georgia*, 8-10.

3. Hodges, *Our Locale*, 181; A. D. Eason account book in possession of A. D. Eason, III, family, Undine, Georgia.

4. Tattnall County Tax Digest, 1850; Eason, *History of Eason's Chapel*, 7; Tattnall County Deed Book DEF: 211.

5. A. D. Eason account book.

6. Ibid.

7. Ibid.

8. The A. D. Eason account book is the reference for all paragraphs in this subheading.

9. Margaret Eason, interview with author, Evans County, Ga., September 20, 2000.

10. Ibid.

Chapter 4 Benjamin "Berry" Brewton House

1. Warren Wilbanks, interview with author, Evans County, Ga., June 30, 2000.

2. *Memoirs of Georgia*, "Tattnall County Sketches," (Easely, S.C.: Southern Historical Press, 1895), 851.

3. Tattnall County Deed Book DEF: 520; Theodore Brewton, interview with Charles P. Johnson, Jr., May 1962 and July 21, 1962, typescript in author's files.

4. Theodore Brewton, interview with Charles P. Johnson, Jr., January 29, 1963, typescript in author's files.

5. *Memoirs of Georgia*, "Tattnall County Sketches," (Easely, S.C.: Southern Historical Press, 1895), 851.

6. Letter, Berrian Brewton to Candace Brewton, Feb. 20, 1864, typescript in author's files.

7. *Memoirs of Georgia*, 851.

8. Wilbanks, interview with author, June 30, 2000.

9. Ibid.

10. Ibid. The other well was on the west side of the porch connecting the house and kitchen.

11. Ibid.

12. Ibid.

13. Ibid.

Chapter 5   Brewton-Hendrix House

1. Tattnall County Deed Book ABCD: 203.

2. John P. Rabun, Jr., *The Jonathan Bacon Brewton House, Evans County, Georgia*, 1996, typescript in author's files.

3. Tattnall County Deed Book E: 275-6; Plat, Tattnall County Deed Book F: 305; Direct General Index to Realty – Tattnall County, Georgia, "Brewton."

4. 1860 Tattnall County Census; Rabun, *Brewton House,* 1996.

5. Lucien Lamar Knight, *Georgia and Georgians*, Vol. VI (New York: The Lewis Publishing Company, 1917), 3207; A. St. Claire-Abrams, *The Manual and Biographical Register of the State of Georgia for 1871-72* (Atlanta: Plantation Publishing Co. Press, 1872); Rabun, *Brewton House,* 1996.

6. Tattnall County Courthouse Probate Records, Inventory and Appraisement of the Estate of Jonathan B. Brewton, Sr., June 23, 1898.

7. "Mystery Farm Site of Former Brick Kiln and Precinct Polling Place," *The Claxton Enterprise*, February 10, 1955.

8. Hodges, *Our Locale,* 39.

9. Wallace Parker, interview with author, Evans County, Ga., July 6, 1995; Cleta McCorkle, interview with author, Evans County, Ga., July 28, 2000. Cleta referred to a conversation with A. D. Eason, III, grandson of A. D. Eason for whom the Eason house was built. Eason told her that Hearn constructed the Brewton House; "Mystery Farm Site of Former Brick Kiln and Precinct Polling Place," *The Claxton Enterprise*, February 10, 1955.

10. McCorkle, interview, July 28, 2000.

11. Ibid.

12. McCorkle, interview, July 28, 2000; Rabun, *Brewton House, 1996.*

13. Evans County Deed Book 15: 576; McCorkle, interview, July 28, 2000.

14. McCorkle, interview, July 28, 2000.

15. These chests are in possession of John P. Rabun, Jr., of Atlanta; Rabun, *Brewton House,* 1996.

Chapter 6   Simon J. Brewton House

1. Nathan's 20 grants comprised 9,573 acres. Original documents are available at Georgia Department of Archives and in Tattnall and Bulloch county records. Photocopies in author's files.

2. Brooks and Leodel Coleman, *The Story of Bulloch* (Statesboro: Bulloch County Historical Society, 1973). In 1861, Simon Brewton, with 6,635 acres, was the fourth largest property owner in Bulloch County; *Savannah Daily News*, October 21, 1865.

3. Bulloch County Probate Office Records, "Simon J. Brewton, 1867 Return of Administrator."

4. Simon Brewton bible entry, photocopy in author's files obtained from Evans County resident Mona Lee Allen.

4. Simon Brewton bible entry, photocopy in author's files obtained from Evans county resident Mona Lee Allen.; Bulloch County Superior Court Minute Book, 1858-1876, 137.

5. Letter, Sallie Brewton to Davidson, Feb. 8, 1928, Vol. 484, Wilcox County DAR Records, 175. Copy at Georgia Department of Archives, Atlanta, Ga.; Bulloch County Superior Court Minute Book, 1858-1876, 137; 1850 Bulloch County Census.

6. Evans County Deed Book 47: 353-4; Bulloch County Deed Book P: 272-3, 2: 143-415, 15: 598-9.

7. Letter, Sallie Brewton to Davidson, Feb. 8, 1928, Vol. 484, Wilcox County DAR Records, 175. Copy at Georgia Department of Archives, Atlanta, Ga.; Bulloch County Superior Court Minute Book, 1858-1876, 137; 1850 Bulloch County Census.

8. Bulloch County Probate Office Estate Records, "Simon Brewton, Return of Perishable Property," June 1866.

9. Peter Strickland, interview with author, Claxton, Ga., November 2, 2000.

10. Bulloch County Probate Office Estate Records, "Simon Brewton, Return of Perishable Property," June 1866.

11. Bulloch County Probate Office Estate Records, "Inventory and Appraisement of the Estate of S.J. Brewton, Deceased," 1866.

Chapter 7   Thomas A. Durrence House

1. George Durrence, "Thomas A. Durrence Patriarch of Family," *The Claxton Enterprise*, March 11, 1954; The family tradition is that Thomas acquired the land in 1858 from his father and built the house soon thereafter. George Durrence, a historian for the family, passed on this date through his newspaper articles and Durrence genealogy book. George probably obtained his information from Herschel Durrence, a longtime owner of the house and son of Thomas A. Durrence. Despite extensive research by the author, however, the date of construction could not be verified through available deed, tax, or court records.

2. George Durrence, *Genealogy of the Durrence Family*, n. p., 1978, 171-2.

3. Tattnall County Tax Digest, 1880; George Durrence, "Thomas A. Durrence Patriarch of Family," *The Claxton Enterprise*, March 11, 1954; 2nd Senatorial District Georgia Militia - District 401 records, Microfilm roll 245-9.

4. 1860 Agricultural Census of Georgia, Tattnall County; Tattnall County Tax Digests, 1859 and 1860.

5. Lucile Hodges, "Our Locale," *The Claxton Enterprise*, March 9, 1950.

6. Tattnall County Estate Records, Thomas A. Durrence will; Evans County Deed Book 43; Durrence, *Durrence Family*, 171-2.

7. Lucile Hodges, "Our Locale," *The Claxton Enterprise*, March 9, 1950.

8. Debra Purcell, interview with author, Claxton, Ga., November 5, 2000.

9. Byron Haire, interview with author, Claxton, Ga., November 5, 2000.

10. Ibid.

11. Lucile Hodges, "Our Locale," *The Claxton Enterprise*, March 9, 1950; Dorothy Durrence Simmons, interview with author, Claxton, Ga., December 12, 2000.

Chapter 8   Edwards-Strickland House

1. Felix Hargrett, *The Edwards Family* (Athens: The Georgian Press, 1984), 15-16. A copy of this limited-edition book is in the Evans County Library genealogical room.

2. Hargrett, *Edwards Family*, 8-9.

3. Letter from John H. Goff to Lucile Hodges, January 6, 1964, Box 2; File 1, Lucile Hodges Papers, Special Collections, Georgia Southern University.

4. Hodges, *Our Locale*, 18.

5. "Roster of Soldiers at Perry's Mills in Tattnall County during War of 1812," reproduced in Hodges, *Our Locale*, facing page 21.

6. *Acts of the General Assembly of the State of Georgia*, November and December 1812, Milledgeville, 1821; For interesting background on Edwards's landholdings see Burkhalter vs. Edwards, *Supreme Court of Georgia Savannah, January term 1855*, 593-600. This volume available in Chatham County, Ga. Courthouse Legal Library.

7. There is no family tradition or other evidence that Edwards replaced his two-story house after 1846.

8. Robert Manson Myers, *Children of Pride* (New Haven: Yale University Press, 1972), 1254, 1257.

9. The 1860 and 1870 Tattnall County censuses lists Edwards's occupation as "doctor."; Hargrett, *Edwards Family*, 20; "W.H. Edwards," *The Albany News*, March 29, 1872.

10. Lillian Whitten, "Daisy Was Another Railroad Town," *The Claxton Enterprise*, August 3, 1989, 43; Evans County Deed Book 1: 224-5, and Deed Book 22: 187-8. Prior to the sale, Deed Book 22 shows the property in the possession of Alline E. Tippins, Lucille E. Herrington, and Mary Lee Everett.

11. Evans County Deed Book 32: 451; J.C. and Julia Strickland, interview with author, Evans County, Ga., July 14, 2000.

12. "Other Towns Once Prospered in Evans Area," *The Claxton Enterprise*, August 3, 1989, 20; Hodges, *Locale*, 161.

13. J.C. and Julia Strickland, interview, July 14, 2000.

14. Ibid.

15. Ibid.

16. Evans County Deed Book 32, 451; Gene Strickland, interview with author, Evans County, Ga., July 14, 2000.

Chapter 9   John Rogers House

1. John Rogers was a member of Captain Crosby's Company at Nails Ferry. Cut off from his unit by the Federal invasion, he was not present when his company surrendered April 1865 at Blackshear, Georgia. "Last Confederate Vet to Live in Evans Co.," *Claxton Enterprise*, July 22, 1938.

2. Samuel Brewton sold the property to Uriah Rogers in 1856. Tattnall County Deed Book A: 512; Deed Book E: 383-384; Deed Book G: 231-232.

3. Harry DeLoach, *Rogers Family, 1775-1983* (Reidsville; Ga., *Tattnall Journal*, 1984), 266.

4. Calvin Durrence, "100 Years of Service to God and Man, 1878-1978, Bull Creek Baptist Church," 1978. Copy in Evans County Library genealogy room.

5. Ibid.

6. Eileen R. Walters, "Old Rogers House," n.d., typescript in author's files.

Chapter 10   Thomas E. Rogers House

1. Harry R. DeLoach, *Rogers Family 1775-1983* (Reidsville, Ga.: *Tattnall Journal*, 1984), 16, 19, 50.

2. Ibid.. 33-36, 50; Tattnall and Bulloch County Land Grant Plat Books; and Tattnall County Deed Books ABCD, DEF and Bulloch County Deed Books FH, FI.

3. Tattnall County tax digests for 1858, 1859, and 1860; and Tattnall County Deed Book DEF, 394.

4. Tattnall County Deed Book DEF, 251 and 259. Hodges, *Locale*, 48-49.

5. Bobbie Jean Todd, interview with author, Evans County, Ga., August 18, 2001; Tattnall County Deed Book W, 459; Evans County deed books 5: 471; 14: 258-259; 52: 11; 83: 585.

6. Thomas E. Rogers, Alexander C. Rogers, Compiled Service Records; 7th Georgia Cavalry website, "History of the 7th," http://www.dreamwater.com/ernieiler/7thGaCav/7th.htm.

7. Bobbie Jean Todd, interview, August 18, 2001.

Chapter 11 Smith-Daniel House

1. Silas Emmett Lucas, Jr., *Index to the Headright and Bounty Grants of Georgia, 1756-1909* (Greenville: Southern Historical Press, Inc. 1982), 609-610.

2. Smith Family Papers, "Families of Evans County," Evans County Library, Claxton, Ga.

3. "Families of Evans County"; Tattnall County Tax Digest, 1843; Hodges, *Locale*, 179-181; Organizers established the campground in 1867. George Durrence, *A History of Tattnall Campground, The Centennial Year, 1867 – 1967* (Reidsville, Ga.: Journal Print, 1967).

4. Tattnall County Deed Book DEF: 235; Mrs. H. C. Hearn, "Fond Memories Part of Bellville's Past," *The Claxton Enterprise*, March 11, 1954. Mrs. Hearn says that Oscar Smith was the first child born in the house. Pulaski Sikes, Oscar's older sibling, was born in 1856 and Oscar, in 1859.

5. Evans County Deed Book 20: 539 and Deed Book 31: 184-5.

6. Jerry Griner, interview with author, Bellville, Ga., August 29, 2000.

7. Hearn, "Fond Memories," 15.

8. Jerry Griner, interview, August 29, 2000. Jerry indicated that during the tin roof replacement with asphalt shingles in 1998, he found remnants of the wood shakes.

9. Ibid.

Chapter 12 Amos Hearn

1. Twiggs County Appraisements, "Appraisement of the goods and Chattels of Jesse Hearn deceased as made by the undersigned this January the 22, 1849"; Jesse Hearn, an Irish immigrant, lived in Rogers's District of Twiggs County. Bess Vaughn Clark, *Twiggs County Georgia Records* (Fernandina Beach: Wolfe Publishing, 1999); Lucile Hodges Papers, Special Collections, Georgia Southern University, Box 2, File 72.

2. A. D. Eason Account Book, in possession of Margaret Eason family, Evans County, Georgia; Tattnall County Tax Digest, 1860; Tattnall County Deed Book F: 147-8.

3. "Mystery Farm Site of Former Brick Kiln and Precinct Polling Place," *The Claxton Enterprise*, February 10, 1955.

4. Tattnall County Tax Digest, 1861.

5. Tim Eason, interview with author, September 20, 2000. This tradition passed to Tim from his father, A. D. Eason, III.

6. Anthony Hearn, "We Moved our Grandfather's Grave," 1956, typescript provided by Emily Hearn Groover. Copy in author's files.

7. Ibid.

GLOSSARY[1]

adze: An axlike tool with a curved blade at right angles to the handle, used for dressing wood.

antebellum: Pre-War Between the States.

auger: A tool for boring holes in lumber.

batten: A narrow board used to cover gaps between siding boards or sheathing; also used to brace and stiffen boards joined edge-to-edge, as in a batten door.

braced framing: A framing system involving the use of corner posts and bracing.

chamfered: A beveled edge on the corner of a post.

cantilever: A projecting beam, girder, or other structural member supported only at one end; used to support a balcony, cornice, extended eaves, or any other extension to a building or structure.

chair rail: A wooden molding that runs along an interior wall at the level of the back of a chair.

clapboard siding: This type of siding consists of boards that are thicker on one edge than the other.

collar beam: A horizontal member that connects two opposite rafters at a level well above the top plate.

column: A pillar, usually circular in plan.

[1] These definitions from the *Old-House Dictionary*, written and illustrated by Steven J. Phillips, (New York: John Wiley and Sons, Inc., 1994). Used by permission of John Wiley & Sons, Inc.

corbelling: A series of projections, each stepped out further that the one below it; most often found on walls and chimney stacks.

dentils: Small square blocks found in series on many cornices, moldings, etc.

Doric order: A classical order characterized by overall simplicity, a plain capital, heavy fluted columns, and no base.

ell: An extension that is at right angles to the length of a building.

engaged columns or rails: A column or rail that is in direct contact with a wall; at least half of the column or rail projects beyond that surface of the wall to which it is engaged.

facade: The principal face or front elevation of a building.

Federal (1780-1830): An architectural style characterized by: overall symmetry, semicircular or elliptical fanlight over a six-panel font door, elaborate door trim, decorated cornice, six-paned double-hung windows arranged most often in five bays, and slender end chimneys.

flue: An enclosed passageway in a chimney for the conveyance of smoke and gasses to the outside.

frame construction: A building consisting primarily or entirely of wood structural members.

froe: A cleaving tool having a heavy blade set at right angles to the handle.

gable: The triangular end of an exterior wall in a building with a roof.

gable roof: A sloping (ridged) roof that terminates at one or both ends in a ridge gable.

Georgian (1700-1780): An architectural style characterized by: symmetry of floor plan and facade, usually gable or gambrel roof, central chimney, roof rectangular lights (panes) in or above the door, flanked by columns or pilasters and capped by a decorative crown or a triangular pediment, and six-pane to twelve-pane double-hung windows.

Greek Revival (1825-1860): An architectural style characterized by: low-pitched gable (or sometimes hipped) roof, a frieze, a pedimented gable, a porch (or portico) with usually nonfluted columns, insignificant chimneys, elongated six-over-six double-hung windows, a four-panel door flanked by side lights with a transom window above, and bevel siding.

joinery: The craft of connecting members together through the use of various types of joints.

joists: Horizontal framing members that run parallel to each other from wall to wall.

lean-to roof: Usually refers to a single-pitch roof that is carried by a higher wall.

molding: A continuous decorative band; serves as an ornamental device on both the interior and exterior of a building or structure.

mortar: A mixture of plaster, cement, or lime with a fine aggregate and water; used for pointing and bonding bricks or stones.

mortise: A rectangular cavity cut in a member; receives a projecting part from another member.

mortise and tenon: A joint composed of a mortise (cavity) and a tenon (projection).

outbuilding: An auxiliary structure that is located away from a house or principal building.

overhang: The part of the roof that extends beyond the wall plane.

pane (or light): A single piece of window glass.

pediment: A triangular section formed by a horizontal molding on its base and two ranking (sloping) moldings on both sides.

piers: Vertical supporting members that are part of the foundation.

pile: Term of measurement used to describe the depth of a building.

pillars: Upright members primarily used for supporting superstructures.

planks: Long heavy pieces of timbers; generally refers to boards six or more inches wide.

plates: Horizontal pieces of timber in a wall used to support rafters, ceiling joists, and other structural members.

rafters: The sloping members of a roof upon which a roof covering is placed.

sash: The framework into which panes are set.

shutters: Solid blinds on either side of a window.

side light: A usually long fixed sash located beside a door or window; often found in pairs.

sill plate: The horizontal member that rests on the foundations and forms the lowest part of the frame of a structure.

summer beam: A large beam that runs from girt to girt and carries one end of the floor joists.

trenail, also trunnel: A wooden peg used to fasten timbers.

tongue and groove: A joint composed of a rib (tongue) received by a groove.

vernacular: The common, functional building type of a period or place (a mode of building based on regional forms and materials).

BIBLIOGRAPHY

Folk and Architectural History

Bishir, Catherine W., and Michael T. Southern. *A Guide to the Historic Architecture of Eastern North Carolina.* Chapel Hill: University of North Carolina Press, 1996.

Bishir, Catherine W., Charlotte V. Brown, Carl R. Lounsbury, and Ernest H. Wood. *Architects and Builders in North Carolina: A History of the Practice of Building.* Chapel Hill: University of North Carolina Press, 1990.

Bonner, James C. *A History of Georgia Agriculture – 1732-1860.* Athens: University of Georgia Press, 1964.

Bush-Brown, Harold. *Outline of the Development of Early American Architecture: The Southern States, District – Georgia*, Atlanta: H.A.B.S., 1936.

Cook, Jody. "Tullie Smith House Restoration: A Realistic Interpretation of The Plantation Plain Style." Master's Thesis, University of Georgia, 1976.

Cooper, Patricia Irvin. "Migration and Log Building in Eastern North Carolina." *Material Culture,* Vol. 31 (1999): 27-54.

Davidson, William H. *Pine Logs and Greek Revival.* Alexander City, Al.: Outlook Publishing, 1965.

Eberlein, Harold Donaldson. *The Architecture of Colonial America.* Boston: Little, Brown, and Company, 1925.

Forman, Henry. *The Architecture of the Old South: The Medieval Style, 1585–1850.* Cambridge, Ma.: Harvard University Press, 1948.

Glassie, Henry. *Pattern in the Material Folk Culture of the Eastern United States.* Philadelphia: University of Pennsylvania Press, 1968.

_____. *Folk Housing in Middle Virginia.* Knoxville: University of Tennessee Press, 1975.

Gowans, Alan. *Images of American Living -- Four Centuries of Architecture and Furniture as a Cultural Expression.* Philadelphia: J.B. Lippincott Company, 1964.

Hale, Jonathan. *The Old Way of Seeing.* Boston: Houghton Mifflin Company, 1994.

Hamlin, Talbot. *Greek Revival Architecture in America.* New York; Dover Publications, Inc.,1944.

Howe, Barbara, Delores Fleming, Emory Kemp, and Ruth Ann Overbeck. *Houses and Homes: Exploring Their History.* Walnut Creek, Ca.: Altamira Press, 1997.

Jackle, John A., Robert W. Bastian, and Douglas Meyer. *Common Houses in America's Small Towns.* Athens: University of Georgia Press, 1989.

Johnson, Frances Benjamin. *The Early Architecture of North Carolina.* Chapel Hill: University of North Carolina Press, 1941.

Kniffen, Fred B. "Folk Housing: Key to Diffusion." *Annals of the Association of American Geographers,* (December 1965), 549-577.

Lane, Mills. *Architecture of the Old South – South Carolina.* Savannah: Beehive Press, 1984.

_____. *The Architecture of the Old South – Georgia.* Savannah: The Beehive Press, 1986.

Lanier, Gabrielle M. and Bernard L. Herman. *Everyday Architecture of the Mid-Atlantic.* Baltimore: Johns Hopkins University Press, 1997.

Light, Sally. *House Histories – A Guide to Tracing the Genealogy of Your Home.* Spencertown, N.Y.: Golden Hill Press, Inc., 1989.

Linley, John. *The Architecture of Middle Georgia – The Oconee Area.* Athens: University of Georgia Press, 1972.

_____. *The Georgia Catalog: Historic American Buildings Survey.* Athens: University of Georgia Press, 1982.

Lounsbury, Carl. "The Building Process in Antebellum North Carolina." *North Carolina Historical Review,* (October 1993), 432-456.

Martin, Van Jones and William Robert Mitchell, Jr. *Landmark Homes of Georgia – 1733-1982*. Savannah: Golden Coast Publishing Company, 1982.

McAlester, Virginia and Lee McAlester. *A Field Guide to American Houses*. New York: Alfred A. Knopf, 1995.

McDonald, Jr., Travis C. "Understanding Old Buildings: The Process of Architectural Investigation." *Preservation Brief 35*, Washington D.C.: National Park Service, 2000.

Nichols, Frederick D. *The Early Architecture of Georgia*. Chapel Hill: The University of North Carolina Press, 1957.

_____. *The Architecture of Georgia*. Savannah: Beehive Press, 1976.

Niles, Andrea and Davina Rochlin. *Architecture in Georgia: The Evolution of the Porch*, Pamphlet series 3, Atlanta: Georgia Trust for Historic Preservation, 1979.

Nye, Russel Blaine. *The Cultural Life of the New Nation*. New York: Harper and Brothers Publishers, 1960.

McKee, Harley. *Recording Historic Buildings*. Washington, D.C.: National Park Service, 1970.

Oliver, Paul, ed. *Encyclopedia of Vernacular Architecture of the World*. Cambridge: Cambridge University, 1997.

Power, Scott, ed. *The Historic Architecture of Pitt County, North Carolina*. Pitt County Historical Society, 1991.

Range, Willard. *A Century of Georgia Agriculture 1850-1950*. Athens: University of Georgia Press, 1954.

Roberts, Warren E. "The Tools Used in Building Log Houses in Indiana." In *Common Places: Readings in American Vernacular Architecture*. eds. Dell Upton and John Vlach. Athens: University of Georgia Press, 1986. 182-203.

Rodgers, Ava D. *The Housing of Oglethorpe County, Georgia 1790-1860*. Tallahassee: Florida State University Press, 1971.

Roller, David, and Robert Twyman, eds. *Encyclopedia of Southern Culture*. Baton Rouge: Louisiana State University Press, 1989.

Sandbeck, Peter B. *The Historic Architecture of New Bern and Craven County North Carolina*. New Bern: The Tryon Palace Commission, 1988.

Robert Matthew Seel, "Nineteenth Century Architectural Survey of Statesboro and Bulloch County, Georgia." Research paper, Clemson University, College of Architecture, April 1988.

Swaim, Doug, ed. *Carolina Dwelling. Toward Preservation of Place: In Celebration of the North Carolina Vernacular Landscape.* Raleigh: North Carolina State University, 1978.

Upton, Dell. "The British Colonies." In *Encyclopedia of the North American Colonies*, Vol. 3. ed. Jacob Ernest Cook. New York: Scribners, 1993.

Wall, Rita Turner. "Genesis of the Southern Plantation House." Statesboro-Bulloch Regional Library. Typescript. County architectural vertical file, n.d.

Whitwell, W. L. and Lee W. Winborne. *The Architectural Heritage of the Roanoke Valley.* Charlottesville: University Press of Virginia, 1982.

Zelinsky, Wilber. "The Greek Revival House in Georgia." *Journal of the Society of Architectural Historians*, XIII, No. 2, (May 1954), 9-12.

Local History

Austin, George F. *One Hundred Years of Methodism in Tattnall County Georgia.* Reidsville, Ga.: Journal Print, 1908.

Brannen, Dorothy, et. al. "Old Houses in Bulloch County: Part 1 – From the Ogeechee to the Canoochee, 19th Century." Typescript. Bulloch County Library, (1978).

_____. *Life in Old Bulloch - The Story of a Wiregrass County in Georgia.* Gainesville, Ga.: Magnolia Press, 1987.

Coleman, Brooks and Leodel Coleman. *The Story of Bulloch.* Statesboro, Ga.: Bulloch County Historical Society, 1973.

Deed Books. Tattnall County: A, B, C, D, E, G; Bulloch County: P, 2, 15; and Evans County: 1, 15, 32, 47.

Durrence, Calvin. "100 Years of Service to God and Man, 1878-1978, Bull Creek Baptist Church." Typescript. Evans County Library, 1978.

Durrence, George. "Thomas A. Durrence Patriarch of Family." *The Claxton Enterprise*, March 11, 1954.

Eason, Annie B. *History of Eason's Chapel United Methodist Church, 1880-1980*. Reidsville, Ga.: *The Tattnall Journal*, n.d.

Eason, A. D. Account book in possession of A. D. Eason, III, family, Undine, Ga.

Georgia Historical Association. "Tattnall County Sketches." *Memoirs of Georgia*. Vol. 1. Atlanta: Georgia Historical Association, 1894.

Hargrett, Felix. *The Edwards Family*. Athens: The Georgian Press, 1984.

Harn, Julia. "Old Canoochee-Ogeechee Chronicles." *Georgia Historical Quarterly*, Part XIII. "Houses." Vol. 25, No. 1, (March 1941), 77-79.

Hearn, Anthony. "We Moved Our Grandfather's Grave." Typescript. 1956.

Hearn, Mrs. H. C. "Fond Memories of Bellville's Past." *The Claxton Enterprise*, March 11, 1954.

Hodges, Lucile. *A History of Our Locale; Mainly Evans County Georgia*. Macon, Ga.: Southern Press, Inc., 1965.

Johnson, Pharris D. *Bellville, Georgia – The First Hundred Years*. Glennville, Ga.: Printech, 1997.

Lucas, Jr., Silas Emmett. *Index to the Headright and County Grants of Georgia, 1756-1909*. Greenville, S.C.: Southern Historical Press, Inc., 1982.

Presley, Delma E. "The Crackers of Georgia." *The Georgia Historical Quarterly*. Vol. 45, (Summer 1976), 102-115.

Rabun, Jr., John P. *The Jonathan Bacon Brewton House*. Typescript. 1996.

_____. *A History of Tattnall County, 1801-1865*. Privately printed, 1954.

Simmons, Dorothy Durrence. *A History of Evans County, Georgia*. Glennville, Ga: Evans County Historical Society, 2000.

_____. *A Durrance-Durrence Family History from England to North Carolina to Wiregrass Georgia*. Glennville, Ga: Printech, 2000.

Walters, Eileen R. "Old Rogers House." Typescript, n.d.

Whitten, Lillian. "Daisy Was Another Railroad Town." *The Claxton Enterprise*. August 3, 1989, 43.

INDEX

Page numbers in italic type refer to illustrations. All place-names are in Georgia unless otherwise indicated.

Traveler's Rest, *2, 9, 16*

Up-and-down saw, 28. *See also* Brewton Mill, Benjamin

Vinson, S. D., 37, 41, 43

War Between the States, 56, 66, 78, 90, 114, 126, 136, 146
Washington, 9, 17
Watkinsville, 9
White House, Major Edward, *19*
White's *Statistics of the State of Georgia,* 28
Wilbanks, Warren, 54, 56-58
Williams House, Thomas, *15*
Wyly, James, 9

Young Carpenter's Assistant, 8